walk with me

Walk with Me

A TRAUMA THERAPIST'S JOURNEY

KELLI HOUGHTON ANDERSON, LCSW
&
TERESA KEARL

The information provided in this book is intended for general public use and should not be construed as a substitute for professional diagnosis or treatment. It is important to note that some professional organizations may hold differing opinions. This book aims to present the available information objectively, without advocating for or against any particular perspective.

Cover photo by Mitchell Orr
Illustrations by Josh Houghton
Substantive editing by Emily Franzen
Copy-editing by River Book Services

ISBN: 978-1-967572-00-7 (Paperback Edition)
ISBN: 978-1-967572-01-4 (Kindle Edition)

Library of Congress Control Number: 2025907091

Published by Grace Notes, LLC
WalkWithKelli.com

1st Edition 2025
Printed in the United States of America

To my amazing tribe who have supported me through the healing transformation.

You know who you are!

To my kiddos—David, Josh, Ben, and Abby—who have been my sunshine since the day they were born!

Along with my bonus kiddos—Carlee, Niki, Paige, and Dallon—who brightened that light.

To my grandson, Simbi, whose hugs and smile make the world seem perfect.

And to my husband, Wayne, for being my bestie and bringing so much love and laughter into my life.

-Kelli

To my favorite people: my husband, children, grandchildren, and their spouses, who know where all the treats are hidden.

To my dear parents who never mistook creativity for naughtiness, and to all my friends—you know who you are.

I'm throwing socks at you!

-Teresa

CONTENTS

CHAPTER 1

LET THE JOY BEGIN

Finding Joy!

As the saying goes, a picture is worth a thousand words. Having worked as a trauma therapist, I never expected to need the same tools I once used to help others on myself, but after devastating trauma, believing in yourself or seeing hope can feel impossible.

The *Storm* that rages during and after trauma can leave you feeling stunned, confused, and directionless—like heavy chains were holding you back. These confounding feelings make relationships, daily routines, and even seemingly simple tasks, like making dinner or picking out an outfit feel overwhelming. Shock can freeze you in place. Doubts and reservations clouded my thoughts. I questioned everything about my past and present, leaving my future uncertain. Thoughts swirled through my mind constantly:

Will I ever feel like myself again?
Will I ever find happiness again?
Is it possible to recover from this?

One summer morning, I headed out on a bike ride with the sole purpose of feeling at peace in nature and intentionally looking for things that brought me joy and gratitude. I chose a path alongside beautiful mountains, where horses grazed in a green field laced with colorful wildflowers, all of which are some of my favorite things. I stopped to take a picture of a flower that brought me joy, capturing the moment. This picture became a symbol of my intentional path to hope, healing and reclaiming peace and joy in my life. This journey can be lonely and difficult, but you do not have to go through it alone.

I would like to accompany you on this journey, so I invite you to -

Walk With Me,

Scan here for a welcome message from Kelli!

CHAPTER 2

INTRODUCTION

Yes, It Is Personal!

It is hard to believe, but trauma can start before you take your first breath. Scientists know that toxic stress experienced during pregnancy shapes a baby's physiological and emotional development before birth.[1] Our physical bodies hold onto trauma until we can acknowledge that what happened to us was terrible and address the internal wounds.[2]

This was the story of my birth. Fear, trauma, and survival have been woven into my existence from the very beginning. My birth father's addiction led him down a reckless and destructive path and eventually he abandoned our family while my mother was pregnant with me. This desertion forced her to fend for herself and care for my older sister, who was still an infant, leaving us vulnerable, unprotected, and exposed to abuse, housing insecurity, and financial instability. His choices left lasting scars that shaped the course of our lives. While my little body was forming, it was molded by the trauma of abandonment and instability.[3] The circumstances of my birth conditioned me to anticipate rejection and withdrawal, leaving my body in a state of high alert to guard against deprivation, rejection, and physical danger before I took my first breath.[4]

Before I could walk, a stepfather entered my life, and my childhood was clouded in bewilderment by unwarranted severity, forced obedience and simmering anger. I constantly struggled to meet his irrational expectations. Any hope of stability was dashed early on and I carry the scars of that relationship to this day. Compounding this distress in my early childhood, extended family battled alcohol dependency and the effects of intergenerational trauma. And yet, in the harshness of these formative years, my innate compassion and desire to nurture and protect others from pain took root. Serving and giving warmth to others brought me peace. Even though I was quite young, my mother recognized my efforts to bring peace and calm to harsh situations.

When I was eight, a wonderful man named Eric adopted me and my sister, and he became our dad. A sea captain by trade, he steered our family out of turbulent waters, removing us from the chaos and unpredictable conditions that surrounded us. He single-handedly changed our course, turning the tide in our family toward stability and love. My dad claimed us as his own, giving us the sense of security, love, and hope we had been missing. He led me down new pathways–from trauma and instability to joy and hope. Dad's part of my journey is close to my heart because he taught me that new stories can be created, and new patterns can be formed.

Professional Background

As a licensed clinical social worker (LCSW) specializing in nonprofit organizations and trauma therapy, I have had a front-row seat to powerful stories of resilience from around the world. I've walked beside individuals as they faced unspeakable trauma, feeling their pain but also witnessing their incredible strength, determination, and resilience. Together, we've navigated the depths of their trauma, guiding them through pain as they acknowledged what had happened to them. I've been by their side as they granted themselves compassion and found new purpose in their lives. Consistently, I've witnessed clients find new strengths, showing that hope, healing, joy, peace, and purpose can and will blossom out of trauma.

It is a privilege to be a voice for the vulnerable and to work with resilient individuals, whether AIDS orphans, sex trafficking survivors, or those who have endured unspeakable hardship. Valuing all life, I am dedicated to "succoring the weak, lifting up the hands which hang down, [and] strengthening the feeble knees,"[5] while encouraging others to "be strong, of good courage, and be not afraid,"[6] thus making the world a safer and better place.

From my youth, some scars of abandonment were etched into my subconscious, influencing my choices and even affecting my body. As an adult, helping others through their trauma made me more aware of my own scars that needed to be healed.[7] Acknowledging my own wounds meant granting myself the compassion I had previously reserved for others. However, ignoring the wounds and scars meant denying myself the same compassion I had given to others. Conceding that certain events in my life were traumatic became part of the healing process. Trauma victims who can look at their choices, feelings, and actions with compassion are crossing the threshold from victim to victor.

Experience shows that there are moments when we help the healing process by supporting others through their difficult challenges. At other times, we are the ones who need help healing. While I naturally prefer helping others, life reminds us that inevitably, we will experience needing help as well as helping others.

Moving from trauma victim to trauma survivor is not easy. In Maya Angelou's wise words, "We delight in the beauty of the butterfly, but rarely admit the changes it has gone through to achieve that beauty."[8] Overcoming trauma requires concentrated effort, patience, self-compassion, and endurance. Nevertheless, every *Storm* passes. There will be a *Clearing.* Rays of light will emerge bringing *Sunshine.* Transformation and peaceful tranquility will break through after every storm.

Sources

1 *Prenatal toxic stress and trauma exposure: Implications for Mental Health professionals.* (n.d.). https://concept.paloaltou.edu/resources/business-of-practice-blog/prenatal-toxic-stress-and-trauma-exposure-implications-for-mental-health-professionals

2 Big Think. (2021, September 19). 6 ways to heal trauma without medication | Bessel van der Kolk | Big Think [Video]. YouTube. https://www.youtube.com/watch?v=ZoZT8-HqI64

3 Teicher, Martin. (2000). Wounds that time won't heal: The neurobiology of child abuse. Cerebrum. 4(2). 50-67.

4 van der Kolk, B. (2014). *The body keeps the score: Brain, mind, and body in the healing of trauma.* Viking.

5 *Doctrine and Covenants 81:5.* (n.d.). https://www.churchofjesuschrist.org/study/scriptures/dc-testament/dc/81?lang=eng

6 *King James Bible (n.d.).* Joshua 1:9

7 Crappy Childhood Fairy. (2022, March 15). Trauma causes emotional dysregulation: Here's how to heal it [Video]. YouTube. https://www.youtube.com/watch?v=4lZ2xTpNiqE

8 A quote by Maya Angelou. (n.d.). https://www.goodreads.com/quotes/84834-we-delight-in-the-beauty-of-the-butterfly-but-rarely

TRAUMA IMPACT PHASES

STORM PHASE

TRAUMATIC IMPACT

DEVASTATION

SURVIVING

CLEARING PHASE

ASSESSING DAMAGE

APPLYING RESOURCES

REBUILDING

SUNSHINE PHASE

POST-TRAUMATIC GROWTH

RENEWAL

THRIVING

STORM PHASE

Traumatic Impact

Devastation

Surviving

CHAPTER 3

TRAUMA IMPACT

An Atomic Bomb

True transformation is an inner journey,
where self-awareness leads to growth
and resilience leads to breakthrough.

— Anonymous

Curled in the fetal position in the smallest corner of my closet, my body was shaking with uncontrollable gasps of breath between sobs. *I never expected to find myself here, as an adult.* The pain of a new reality was paralyzing and earth-shattering, as if my entire being had been crushed into a million shards of glass that would never be put back together again. As time passed, I referred to this as the moment my body broke—but it was much more than my body. It was my entire existence. Every breath sliced through me, the jagged and splintered pieces of myself cutting deeper. Everything in my world had just been turned upside down and inside out.

My mind was swirling back and forth in phases of denial. *This is too much. This is not real. This cannot be happening.* It felt as if my connection to everything was severed. Still unable to catch my breath, I wondered why the pain couldn't just stop. The natural desire to breathe was exhausting. And then, in a matter of seconds, like a vulture waiting for the right moment to land, the darkest feeling of hopelessness descended with a force and immediacy that was even more shocking. I knew nothing at that moment. I would never be myself again. Lost. Cast away. Drifting. Everything normal thirty minutes before—gone.

Painful Irony

In this chaos, the therapist in me remained, recognizing the clinical process taking place in my body, but the sheer intensity of the physical pain and emotional distress blindsided me. It is a bitter irony that my work became my experience. In private practice, my specialty is helping others work through trauma. I've stood at the bedside of emergency room patients whose lives were permantetly altered. I've given presentations on overcoming trauma. Having experienced trauma early in my life, I thought I was well prepared for any type of challenge. And yet, that knowledge and experience could not shield me from—or prepare me for the soul-shattering intensity of the day my body broke. Everything I knew became unrecognizable. My trauma *Storm* shattered who I had been. I refer to this moment as *the atomic bomb.*

The details and specific circumstances of my traumatic experience are not crucial to this book, and it is of note that recounting traumatic experiences is not required for the healing process.[1] What *is* crucial is my personal journey from a devastated, broken soul in the corner of a closet, overcome with hopelessness, to intentionally choosing hope and healing. This purposeful shift from trauma victim to survivor and then to thriving victor developed a desire inside of me to "fight like hell for peace and joy." So much had been taken from me through this trauma that I made an intentional decision not to allow peace and joy to be stolen from me again. While necessary to heal, this decision did not spare me from trauma's natural responses. Changing circumstances, outcomes, and healing all require hard work.

Trauma is a thief and a disrupter. During the *Storm Phase* trauma may rob or strip you of your security, your past, your present, or your future. Confronting trauma is the fight to preserve your life and your sanity. Holocaust survivor and therapist Dr. Viktor Frankl emphasized that facing our suffering head-on will help us overcome our challenges with fortitude, strength, and perseverance. Additionally, the more difficult the obstacle, the more resilient humans become without regard to age, economic status, gender, or the type of trauma.[2]

Unfortunately, even as a trauma therapist, my body would have to go through all the natural trauma responses and healing processes, just as an orthopedic surgeon would have to after shattering his or her own leg. Knowing the process of healing a broken leg does not shield a doctor from experiencing the pain of the process, and it was the same in my case. Regardless of my knowledge and experience, I was not exempt from the physical and emotional pain of rebuilding and overcoming trauma. According to Dr. Bessel van der Kolk, the first step in overcoming past trauma is developing physical self-awareness to help you recognize how your body reacts to sensations and emotions.[3] This healing process is challenging, with highs and lows, setbacks, and obstacles. Some events leave life-altering wounds. It is an exhausting process. It can feel overwhelming and very lonely. All of this is normal, and if you are feeling this, you are doing just fine. I want to assure you, that these painful events can bring silver linings, such as hidden strength of character, resilience, profound empathy, and new depths of wisdom. As both a trauma survivor and therapist, I have witnessed this silver lining in my own journey and those I help.

Here's a little garden parable for you:

> *After planting some beautiful bell pepper plants in what seemed like the perfect spring, my rows of peppers were thriving. Then, an unusually hot wind came and stayed for days. Despite watering the garden twice a day and protecting each plant with coverings, all of the pepper plants were burned. It was too late in the season to start all over, and garden nurseries were sold out of bell peppers. I was a little heartsick at the thought of losing this part of my garden and having no peppers for fall preserves.*
>
> *If there was a chance to save these plants, I had to start at the bottom. Crawling on my hands and knees, I dug up each plant, inserting water retention fabric and gel beneath the roots. After trimming all the burned leaves and stems, the plants looked like twigs when I finished. The plants not only rebounded but everywhere they were cut, they sprouted two new stems in the place of the old single stem. This resulted in the largest pepper harvest I've ever had. What initially seemed destroyed and burned beyond hope turned*

into an unexpectedly wonderful harvest with work, patience, and attention—becoming the best I can remember.[4]

Like the pepper plants that were burned and then pruned, new growth takes time to become visible. Overcoming trauma takes time. Clients have expressed that while they would not want to relive their trauma *Storm,* they were grateful for the changes and growth that have given them new and bountiful harvests in their personal lives. The goal is not *mere endurance* as we navigate adversity; the goal is to strengthen our best traits and grow in ways we never thought possible.

For as long as I have been on my healing journey, I still have moments that land me in dark spaces. But with the reminder of my personal mantra, "I will fight like hell for peace and joy," I am able to focus on joy and peace and continue to grow in new directions.

I believe that putting peace and joy together brings empowerment. In the following chapters, Teresa and I will share resources, coping skills, and examples, along with my personal journey. We hope to provide ideas on how to move from surviving to thriving and how to intentionally transform trauma into hope and healing. While trauma can result from a single event or a series of events, for the sake of clarity, we will refer to it as the trauma *Storm* or *Storm Phase* throughout this work. We hope that by the end of the book, you will have discovered ways to magnify peace, joy, and empowerment in your own life and will be inspired to share the knowledge you've learned with those in your circle.

This book is for anyone on this journey of healing. Trauma can be categorized into *Trauma Impact Phases: Storm, Clearing,* and *Sunshine.* Whether you're just beginning in the *Storm Phase,* in the midst of the *Clearing Phase* or well along the path headed towards the *Sunshine Phase,* there is no right or wrong pace, only your own. There are no expectations. No matter how alone or wounded you feel, there is hope ahead. There are peaceful and joyful days in your future. This was never written as a step-by-step guide, but rather as a wayfinding map, offering different routes toward the destination of "Hope and Healing." A Turkish proverb says, "A good companion shortens the longest road."[5]

Trauma is a long road, but you don't have to take this journey alone. I invite you to walk with me.

Activities

1. Write down and identify specific moments you felt broken.
2. Create your own mantra about your journey or goal. It doesn't have to be poetic or pretty, but bonus points for you if it is. Remember mine was "fight like hell for peace and joy."
3. Using our garden parable, create a parable about a plant, a tree, a rose bush, or any type of vegetation. Explain how a traumatic experience nearly killed it. Then imagine a happy future, writing or drawing about the process, work, and transformation to get there, giving as many details as possible. Write about your experience and how your garden thrived after the devastation.

Sources

1 Contreras, A. (2024, July 21). Exploring common myths we've believed to be true about healing trauma effects. *Psychology Today.* https://www.psychologytoday.com/us/blog/traumatization-and-its-aftermath/202407/5-myths-about-healing-from-trauma

2 Buckingham, M. (2021, August 30). *What really makes us resilient?* Harvard Business Review. https://hbr.org/2020/09/what-really-makes-us-resilient

3 van der Kolk, B.A. (2014). *The body keeps the score: brain, mind, and body in the healing of trauma.* https://ci.nii.ac.jp/ncid/BB19708339. p.101

4 Kearl, T. Personal experience.

5 *The Wisdom of the Kurds 100 Proverbs* https://d2fahduf2624mg.cloudfront.net/pre_purchase_docs/BK_OASI_001410/2020-06-24-05-22-29/bk_oasi_001410.pdf. (n.d.). Retrieved December 5, 2024

CHAPTER 4

THE FIRST STEP

A Decision to Rebuild

In any moment of decision, the best thing you can do is the right thing,
the next best thing is the wrong thing,
and the worst thing you can do is nothing.

— Theodore Roosevelt

Walking through the different phases of trauma, the path ahead is usually unclear and can feel daunting! That is why it is crucial to find evidence around us that, with time and effort, recovery is tangible, and a meaningful life can be rebuilt.

Throughout history, we've seen stunning structures fall, only to rise again even more magnificent than before. The reclamation and restoration of France's Notre-Dame Cathedral, the White House, St. Paul's Cathedral in London, the Claremont Hotel in San Francisco, Dresden, Germany's Frauenkirche, and even entire cities like Chicago, San Francisco, and London stand as a testament to the human ability to restore and rebuild. These landmarks, which represented the work and lives of generations, were destroyed by fire, war, and earthquakes but each was rebuilt.[1]

These grand buildings, cities, and churches connect us to our history. They represent the work, artistry, ingenuity, sacrifice, and lives of those who came before us. When they fall, it seems a bitter, irreplaceable loss. These landmarks have been rebuilt, each rebuilt in a unique way and on different timelines.

On April 15, 2019, the Notre-Dame Cathedral of Paris caught fire, destroying centuries of history. As of this writing, the cathedral has reopened after an incredible restoration that has been completed in under five years. This monumental effort has ensured that the cathedral will continue to bless and uplift visitors from around the world, offering beauty and peace as a place of worship.[2]

The United States' White House was rebuilt in 1817, after its destruction in 1814, and continues to be a significant symbol of the United States.[3] St. Paul's Cathedral in London, originally completed in 1710, was damaged by bombing during World War II; but it is now rebuilt and is now lit to celebrate the remarkable human resilience.[4] Dresden's Frauenkirche, known for its ornate, baroque period architecture, was destroyed by bombing raids during World War II. The plans to rebuild did not commence until 1994. This was almost fifty years after its destruction. The rebuilding required a committee of people who were invested in the project and had the patience and fortitude to rebuild and restore what had been lost for so long. Reopening just eleven years later, Bishop Jochen Bohl said at the church's first sermon, "A deep wound that has bled for so long can be healed."[5]

As structures, cities, and cathedrals can be restored, so too can the human spirit. Studies have shown that almost everyone experiences trauma at least once in their lifetime.[6] Whether the trauma response is triggered by a death, betrayal, crime, tragic accident, medical emergency, or any other situation, life's challenges can leave each of us damaged and wounded with holes in our souls and scars on our bodies.

We each handle trauma in our own way. It is important for everyone going through any type of trauma, including the "hole in your soul" type, to keep these things in mind:

- **Your decision to recover is the first step**
- **Recovery from Trauma is possible** as your brain, body, and soul are designed to heal
- **Your scars will serve as a sign of your strength and resilience as you heal**
- **The journey to recovery is personal** and will not look the same for anyone

- **The recovery process isn't linear** as there will be ups and downs and unexpected twists and turns, but recovery is possible
- **Recovery is a personal decision.** While others may help, you *decide when to begin and which tools and resources best fit your needs*

As you take your first step in this journey to recovery and rebuilding, know that your journey is yours alone - but you are not alone! Along the way, you may find support groups, therapists, good friends, healing literature, creative hobbies, and self-care practices. The challenges ahead are real, but as you work through the *Trauma Impact Phases,* they will take you out of the *Storm,* through the *Clearing* and into the *Sunshine* once again.

Activities

1. Watch videos online of structures being rebuilt.
2. Visit a site that has been renewed.
3. Write down or draw what you want your life to look like when you are rebuilt.

Sources

1 Insider. (2019, April 26). *8 famous buildings around the world that were rebuilt after devastating events.* Business Insider. https://www.businessinsider.com/famous-buildings-rebuilt-after-devastating-events-2019-4

2 Friel, M., & Rennolds, N. (2024, November 29). *Photos show inside the rebuilt Notre Dame Cathedral ahead of its reopening.* Business Insider. https://www.businessinsider.com/photos-rebuilt-notre-dame-cathedral-2024-11

3 White House Historical Association. (n.d.). *Rebuilding the White House.* WHHA (en-US). https://www.whitehousehistory.org/construction-of-the-white-house/rebuilding-the-white-house

4 St. Paul's Cathedral. (n.d.). *Wartime damage and repair.* St Paul's Cathedral. https://www.stpauls.co.uk/wartime-damage-and-repair

5 Welle, D. (2005, October 29). Landmark Dresden Church completes rise from the Ashes. *dw.com.* https://www.dw.com/en/landmark-dresden-church-completes-rise-from-the-ashes/a-1758986

6 *Statistics for Mental Trauma | How Common is it & Who it Affects.* (n.d.). FHE Health. https://fherehab.com/trauma/statistics

CHAPTER 5

WHAT IS TRAUMA?

Stuck Between a Rock and a Hard Place

Out of suffering have emerged the strongest souls;
the most massive characters are seared with scars.

— Khalil Gibran

Your trauma may feel like a slow boil, where repeated manipulation or bullying grips you in continuous fear, as though you are dangling off the edge of a cliff, waiting to fall. Or it may feel as though you were suddenly pushed off a cliff without warning. Either way, trauma can leave victims feeling as though they are stuck between a rock and a hard place.

The Four Fs

My traumatic experience came on suddenly, without warning, leaving me no way to prepare for the sudden change in my life. There was no way to avoid it, escape, or insulate myself from the atomic bomb. I felt I had no choice in the event which worsened the compounding stress. I experienced what is commonly called "The Four Fs".[1] The Four Fs stand for the physical and emotional responses to trauma; *fight, flight, freeze or fawn.* In my case, I wanted to run and hide which would be classified as a flight response.

In consideration of my experience with trauma, and some of my clients, I recognize how powerful the lack of choice can be. In 2015, neuroscientist Steven Maier discovered through neuroimaging that having some element of choice during traumatic or negative events can help buffer and reduce vulnerability, building resilience against future trauma. On the other hand, a lack of choice during a detrimental event can amplify a traumatic response.[2] Based on my personal experience with trauma and my professional work, I agree that choice-or the lack of it-plays a significant role in how trauma develops. However, trauma can also arise from making poor choices, faulty judgment-causing harm to others, or other regrettable decisions.

A traffic accident, cancer, a death, the loss of a position at work, a medical emergency, divorce, loss of a limb, a serious romantic breakup, a betrayal, a physical or sexual assault, and many other events can bring on a trauma response. Any type of severe and sudden event causes the amygdala in the brain to release higher amounts of cortisol and adrenaline hormones which prime the body for a fight, flight, freeze, or fawn responses. If you are interested in understanding anxiety that can onset from a large hormone release, Chapter 12 or "My Anxiety has Anxiety" of this book, addresses the physical and emotional responses to anxiety in greater detail.

Trauma and Perception

While trauma influences our body's reaction, it can also impact our perception of the world around us, and ourselves. Trauma shapes how we think, respond, and react due to chemical changes in the brain.[3] These reactions stem from perceived threats, past experiences, and individual bodily responses, and are driven by a natural instinct for self-protection.[4] Whether caused by a series of events that gradually break you or a single traumatic moment, trauma reshapes the body and mind, redefining how the world looks. As the *Storm Phase* progresses—characterized by heightened emotional and physical responses-those affected by trauma may be on high alert when engaging in the world, hyper-focused on self-preservation. Increased sensitivity to surroundings, interactions, images, smells, or sounds -known as trauma triggers- can emerge. Trauma redefines what physical, emotional, spiritual, or financial security means.

Trauma can affect your outlook by changing what was once a positive belief into an accusatory or self-defeating belief.

Positive Beliefs such as:

- *I am strong*
- *I am enough*
- *I can try again*
- *I can work hard*
- *I can overcome obstacles*
- *I am capable*
- *I am safe*
- *I have value*
- *I deserve success*
- *I play vital role in others' lives*

May be replaced by more self-defeating, negative beliefs such as:

- *I am weak*
- *I am not in control*
- *I don't have a choice*
- *I should give up*
- *I am not good enough*
- *I am a disappointment*
- *There is no way out*
- *I am hopeless*

- *This is unfixable*
- *I am in danger*
- *I am dumb*
- *I let everyone down*
- *I will never succeed at anything*

When that shift causes one to adopt a negative belief mindset, a person's body starts to aggressively protect itself. The physical and emotional impact can trigger PTSD, anxiety, and depression. The more we learn and study about trauma experiences, the more we understand how trauma can negatively impact the whole body. Mental health and physical well-being cannot be separated. Our physiological responses are merely natural, instinctive, and protective human responses.

Trauma can occur at any phase of life and in any setting. As a therapist, I've worked with clients who felt trauma made them lose control, whether from regret over an unchangeable decision, a mistake they or someone else made, or from natural causes. Regardless of the cause, trauma results when the body and mind feel physically or emotionally threatened and unprotected. Essentially, it occurs when our safe expectations meet the edge of a cliff, and we see no way out. We are stuck, without options, *between a rock and a hard place.*

Whether you feel as if you are caught in the fallout of an atomic bomb, without a safety zone, or you feel as if you stepped over a cliff, falling off what felt like solid ground, or the shock of a hard crash landing can evoke a trauma response when we either anticipate the pain ahead or replay the traumatic event over and over. Trauma can stem from replaying the survival experience itself—when life as you know it collapses around you, and yet you survive, but survival does not always bring relief. This is where our bodies and minds can become stuck in a cycle of hypervigilance or fear. This can lead to anxiety and depression, as the four Fs take over. When things are destabilized around you, without an escape plan or a safe passage through the event or events, fight, flight, freeze, or fawn become instinctive ways we attempt to protect ourselves.[5]

Avoid Negative Comparisons

It is important to remember that trauma has so many variables, the same experience can have varying degrees of impact on individuals. Avoid negative comparisons of yourself or anyone else. Chronic illness, death, abandonment, infertility, relationship changes, abuse, broken dreams, or a myriad of other life events affect everyone differently. No two people experience the same trauma in the same way. Two people could be in the same car accident, but one person may be able to cope and process the event and bounce back quickly while the other individual's body has a trauma response. That second individual may even experience trauma to the point that they have difficulty getting back in a car after the accident. Experiencing trauma is not a sign of weakness or a character flaw. Rather, it is a sign your mind is trying to protect you. Give yourself grace by avoiding comparisons and beating yourself up.

All four of my children were born by cesarean section, giving me an up close and personal understanding of the intense pain felt the first time a nurse assists you out of bed to walk after the surgery. It is a specific pain that is difficult to explain until someone has experienced it. The level of pain and intensity even within the same experiences will be to different degrees due to internal and external conditions. For instance, how much pain medicine is still in the body, prior painful experiences someone has experienced, pain tolerance level, the nurse's personality, family support, physical assistance devices, etc.

Healing from trauma may seem impossible, or even overwhelming, but remember life will get better. Our bodies and minds are designed to heal. As you make an intentional transformation, traumatic images and memories will begin to lose their jagged and sharp edges. Life will become more manageable as you gain skills, tools, and beneficial adaptive behaviors that restore control. In time, you will see yourself in a new light. The *Storm Phase* of trauma, just like a regular storm, will pass. There is a *Clearing* ahead. No one has to remain a permanent victim, a target, or a scapegoat.

You may think of life in different periods; life before trauma and life after trauma. Although this turning point comes with wounds, scars, pain, and change — it also brings new strength. Healing is not a straight path, but you are moving forward, every day you are closer to reclaiming and restoring your life. Hold on—there is hope and healing ahead!

Activities

1. Identify areas you do not feel in control of. Why?
2. Which negative beliefs have you said about yourself?
3. What positive beliefs do you want to have instead? Then start to practice replacing negative beliefs with your positive beliefs.

Sources

1 *The 4F's of trauma response: fight, flight, freeze, and fawn.* (2024, October). Therapy Trainings. Retrieved December 23, 2024, from https://www.therapytrainings.com/pages/blog/the-4-fs-of-trauma-response-fight-flight-freeze-and-fawn

2 CU Boulder Today. (2015, December 2). Longtime CU-Boulder professor wins prestigious Grawemeyer Award. https://www.colorado.edu/today/2015/12/02/longtime-cu-boulder-professor-wins-prestigious-grawemeyer-award

3 van der Kolk, B.A. (2014). *The body keeps the score: Brain, Mind, and Body in the Healing of Trauma.* pp.157-159. Penguin.

4 Guy-Evans MSC, O. G. (2023, November 9). *Fight, flight, freeze, or fawn: How we respond to threats.* Simply Psychology. https://www.simplypsychology.org/fight-flight-freeze-fawn.html

5 WordToTheWise. (2019, June 26). How to Beat Fear and Anxiety | Jordan Peterson | Powerful Life Advice [Video]. YouTube. https://www.youtube.com/watch?v=bb9g9mtDHZo

CHAPTER 6

PHYSICAL IMPACT

Letting the Cat Out of the Bag

It takes courage to live through suffering, and it takes honesty to observe it.

— C.S. Lewis

In the months following my traumatic experience, I was still undergoing an active trauma response. I felt physically weak, like my life was slipping away or flickering out, and I didn't have the strength or ability to stop it. It seemed like no part of my body, inside or out, was left untouched! Many friends and family noticed and commented during the *Storm* and *Clearing Phases* that I had lost my light; they said I didn't look like myself. The release of stress hormones, the sympathetic nervous system activation, and other changes in your body can initiate a cascade of physical responses.[1] Moreover, while it is not scientifically proven, it is difficult not to wonder if the cascade of physical responses adds to a disjointed sense of time. During traumatic events, time can feel as if it is suspended or slowed beyond reason, a phenomenon known as time slippage. When you are physically suffering, time slows down, making minutes feel like hours, and days feel like weeks. In addition to the strange relationship with time, when you don't feel physically well, even the simplest of tasks like cleaning, shopping, paying bills, can feel overwhelming and impossible.

To better understand the physiological impact of trauma, consider the findings from the National Institute of Health:

Reactions to trauma can include exhaustion, confusion, sadness, anxiety, agitation, numbness, dissociation, physical arousal, and blunted affect. Indicators of more severe responses include continuous distress without periods of relative calm or rest, severe dissociation symptoms, and intense intrusive recollections that continue despite a return to safety. Delayed responses to trauma can include persistent fatigue, sleep disorders, nightmares, fear of recurrence, anxiety focused on flashbacks, depression, and avoidance of emotions, sensations, or activities that are associated with the trauma, even remotely.[2]

A trauma *Storm* can impact the body in numerous physical ways.[3] It can also set off an inflammatory response and disruptions in the cardiovascular, respiratory, or digestive systems.[4] I personally experienced many of these symptoms. One night the intensity of the trauma became overwhelming. With thoughts racing, I began shaking uncontrollably in almost seizure-like symptoms. Then a desperate, choking cry overtook me. I couldn't get out of bed due to the intense shaking. I have always been able to calm myself, so the inability to calm my physical response increased the fear and despair I felt. As a strong woman who has faced challenges—living in the harsh extremes of Alaska, traveling to developing countries, and helping others through traumatic experiences—the physical repercussions of my trauma caught me completely off guard. It was staggering, unexpected, and scary. This aspect of a traumatic experience is challenging to explain to someone who has not been through something similar. It is not that others don't believe you; it is just difficult to explain the depth of the physical response to traumatic events without firsthand knowledge. I now realized in a deeper way what my clients had gone through.

That night home alone, I experienced a combination of symptoms all at once, sobbing, shaking, unraveling. Surviving the initial atomic bomb was one thing, enduring the aftermath was another, and nothing prepared me for the raw intensity of physical anguish. I felt the crushing weight of misery, engulfed by hopelessness. As the night went on, my tears kept coming like the waves of a tsunami. The shaking and tremors grew worse with each passing moment. I thought about calling someone for help. Glancing at the clock, it was too late. Even if it wasn't too late, I couldn't bring myself to bother anyone.

That night I was drowning in isolation, broken and out of control. Trauma does that—it convinces you to suffer in silence, to hold everything in. Hours passed—shaking, gasping for air—one of the longest nights of my entire life, until exhaustion finally won out. If you've been blindsided by trauma's pain, know this: the shockwaves are real.

When you are experiencing the hardship of a traumatic event, it is normal to be surrounded by your best friends and loving family and yet still feel isolated. From time to time, friends and family expressed concern. "Hey, are you okay? You can call me anytime." Unfortunately - No, I was not okay. I felt unsafe and shaken, as if the world was spinning out of control. During the *Storm Phase,* it was often too difficult to share how I really felt with so much change, chaos, and danger in the air.

The New Normal

Trauma and stress take a toll on appetite. Some people lose their appetite completely, and the thought of food makes them nauseous. Others report increased cravings. Persistent nausea replaced my appetite. Changes in appetite are a normal response to stress or trauma. These changes are not a cause for concern. As you work through the trauma response, your appetite should return to normal, although it may take some time. If the changes persist beyond six to eight weeks, seek help to avoid developing an eating disorder or other serious conditions.

As a result of stress and nausea, my weight dropped significantly, my hair began falling out, and my body was swollen with inflammation. While hair loss is a normal reaction to stress, watching it fall out by the handful does not feel normal—it only amplified my anxiety. The domino effect of my trauma spilled over into all areas of my life, intensifying the physical and emotional toll. The physical changes were disheartening as I felt like I was losing control over my energy, my appetite, and even my hair. The effects of trauma were manifesting physically, heightening my emotions, anger, and frustrations.

Health Decline

As my emotional distress deepened, it became impossible to ignore the physical effects. While in the *Storm* and *Clearing Phases,* my health took a noticeable turn. For the first time in my life, I had high blood pressure, became pre-diabetic, and struggled with the effects of increased inflammation. A chronic twitch developed in one eye, and my normally sound sleep became restless and sporadic. Due to a combination of sleep disturbances and my red, swollen eyes from daily crying, I barely recognized myself. My well-managed chronic conditions became problematic, spiraling out of control.

This pattern of health changes is not unusual. Many of my clients navigating through the *Storm* and *Clearing Phases* of traumatic experiences suffer from sudden (acute) or ongoing persistent (chronic) physical symptoms. Renowned trauma researcher and author Dr. Gabor Maté warns that emotional stress is a major contributor to physical illness. The physical and hormonal systems that regulate emotions are directly linked to the nervous and immune systems. Emotional regulation structures are intertwined with all our physical and immunological systems, affecting each other.[5] The big secret—letting the cat out of the bag—is that every system of the body is connected. Trauma doesn't stay contained; it manifests itself every possible way, both physically and emotionally.

Critical Priority Triage

The physical and emotional part of the healing journey takes time. Trauma recovery needs to be triaged as if it were a major medical crisis. When a trauma patient is in an emergency room, there are specific steps and an order of care to follow. The most urgent, logistical, and lifesaving steps need to come first, and treatment continues from there. We can't do everything at once. We need to look at the healing process as phases of recovery and have patience as we prioritize those phases one at a time. For example, when a loved one passes away, handling funeral arrangements, settling financial matters, and notifying agencies of passing take precedence over other things. In my case, I had to delay

addressing my physical concerns, until I had triaged more important priorities. Whatever your traumatic experience, I recommend making a list of priorities and reviewing it daily. I found that to be incredibly helpful.

Just as medical patients are evaluated by first ensuring safety, and identifying the most critical situations or needs, it is essential to prioritize tasks from most urgent to least critical. When you are in the midst of a trauma *Storm Phase,* safety is the first priority. In my case, I had to put my physical health several steps down the path as I had other pieces that were more urgent and necessary to settle before focusing on more in-depth health treatments. One thing I learned, that even though there were things I would have liked to have done right at the beginning— I knew when the more urgent items were managed, I would be able to focus on deeper physical healing. This is key. As resilient humans, we learn to adapt to our injuries. We may never return to our previous life, health, or living situations, but we can find strength and happiness in our new circumstances. Recovering from the physical toll takes time. We cannot command our bodies and minds to immediately recover, but with time and effort, we do recover.

If you have any life-threatening physical symptoms, please seek professional help immediately. We live in a world with many options. Most are a combination of treatments that work well for each of us individually. Yours may be exercise, medication, and nutrition. Others may feel stronger through intense therapy, nutrition, and by adding a new hobby. The challenge in overcoming the physical response to trauma is searching for the specific processes that are geared toward your personal needs.

Intentional Recovery

When the time was right, I spent time researching a healing path forward. For me, this path included modern medicine, along with ancient medicine, exercise, and nutrition. Much of my motivation was the desire to no longer allow trauma to have control over my body. This required intentional planning to reduce my acute and chronic symptoms.

As I have continued my healing journey working through the *Trauma Impact Phases* of *Storm, Clearing* and *Sunshine,* the same family and friends who expressed concern with my physical changes during the *Storm* and *Clearing Phases* have mentioned, "You look like your old self" or "Kelli is back." The physical healing from trauma is the same as any recovery after a physical injury. Healing takes place from the inside out. Even after healing, the physical scars and injuries of trauma can linger.[6]

A friend of mine fell, damaging her hip and thigh. Although she had surgery to repair the damage years ago, she refers to the pain in her hip as a weather station—it predicts storms. Just like her hip, emotional injuries, even though healed, serve as a warning system and may even predict storms.

Healing from trauma is exhausting. Even writing about it drains my energy. Rebuilding health and strength is essential in the healing process. And while the timeline is unpredictable, each step, no matter how small, moves the mind and body towards recovery.

I would like to leave this chapter with a story of hope and healing. Jami Bollschweiler intentionally changed her life after a trauma *Storm*. She found recovery unexpectedly behind the lens of a camera. Sharing her story, she began to photograph wildlife as a way to heal from devastating trauma. She didn't expect to become a world-famous photographer. Spending time in nature allowed her body and mind to heal. While she was working on triaging her very personal wounds, Jami also honed her photography talents and spent countless hours sitting in the mud and dirt of sun-scorched plains. Her tenacity paid off as she captured incredible wildlife scenes that include once- in- a-lifetime moments of wild horses in the western desert. Her photos have been published worldwide.[7] Like Jami, I found that healing is not only about moving on. Healing is an intentional journey forward. Her resilience is a reminder that the scars of trauma open new pathways. Jami's healing journey, and those of my many clients demonstrate that the hard work of healing often leads to something greater than we imagine, reinforcing my belief that anyone who seeks healing *will find it*—and more.

Activities

1. Create a daily priority list by answering: What are the most pressing or urgent tasks that require attention today?
2. Identify your physical symptoms and write out a plan with specific goals of how you will work to reduce the symptoms.
3. Reflect on how you have managed your physical symptoms and write a short sentence about it.

Sources

1 Fitzpatrick, J. (2024, November 8). *How trauma affects the body: Understanding the physical impact and healing approaches — Hopeology*. Hopeology. https://www.hopeologypsych.com/blog/trauma-and-the-body-how-trauma-affects-physical-health-and-healing

2 Center for Substance Abuse Treatment (US). Trauma-Informed Care in Behavioral Health Services. Rockville (MD): Substance Abuse and Mental Health Services Administration (US); 2014. (Treatment Improvement Protocol (TIP) Series, No. 57.) Chapter 3, Understanding the Impact of Trauma. Available from: https://www.ncbi.nlm.nih.gov/books/NBK207191/

3 Fitzpatrick, J. (2024, November 8). *How trauma affects the body: Understanding the physical impact and healing approaches — Hopeology*. Hopeology. https://www.hopeologypsych.com/blog/trauma-and-the-body-how-trauma-affects-physical-health-and-healing

4 Enabnit, A., & Warren, A. (2023, July 22). *Physiology of Trauma: Understanding the body's response to injury - DoveMed* (K. Tangella MD, MBA, Ed.). DoveMed. Retrieved January 1, 2025, from https://www.dovemed.com/health-topics/focused-health-topics/physiology-trauma-understanding-bodys-response-injury

5 Maté, G. (2024, August 9). *Addiction expert, speaker and best-selling author Dr. Gabor Maté*. Dr. Gabor Maté. https://drgabormate.com/

6 Van Der Kolk, B. (2015). *The body keeps the score: Brain, Mind, and Body in the Healing of Trauma*, pp.2-3. Penguin Books.

7 Bollschweiler, Jami, (2025) Personal Interview by Teresa Kearl. See also *Jami Bollschweiler Official website*. (n.d.). Jami Bollschweiler - Official Website. https://jami-bollschweiler.pixels.com/

CHAPTER 7

EMOTIONAL IMPACT

Typical Reactions to an Atypical Experience

People who have been through trauma, their souls are hurting.

— Mary Gauthier

The *Storm Phase* of trauma can feel destructive. Like a tornado, it can upend familiar routines, leaving your emotional world unrecognizable. Previously safe and comfortable thoughts and emotions are replaced by desolate, foreign feelings and reactions, leaving you unsteady on your feet. Adding to this, thought processes may feel jumbled and confused, causing you to doubt your feelings and emotions. This can leave you wary of new situations and feeling completely helpless.

Unrecognizable

At this point in my *Storm Phase,* the world did not make sense. *Was this a bad dream? This had to be a bad dream.* It felt as if I were living in a different dimension. It was as if I were seeing a cow above my head and a house swirling in the air. The solid things in life were no longer anchored to reality. Nothing was as it should be. Life was unrecognizable.

As you begin to see the effects of the *Storm,* it is very much like splintered beams and wreckage barreling toward you during a tornado. They come fast and are too much for your mind to process. During my traumatic *Storm,* the emotions unfolded quickly, leaving me overwhelmed and exhausted. Much like a computer when it locks up due to a lack of processing power, you may get the "spinning wheel of death." Overwhelming trauma may cause your brain to feel stuck and unable to process or move forward. When I experienced this brain freeze, I would forget appointments, lose track of what I was doing or saying, struggle to form sentences, and repeatedly check to see what day it was. This was highly atypical of my usual behavior, yet reactions like this are completely normal in the *Storm Phase.* This is called emotional dysregulation.[1]

Trauma-based emotional dysregulation makes it difficult to process and regulate emotional responses after trauma. It can lead to overwhelming emotions such as intense sadness, anger, or anxiety, which can be hard to control. During the *Storm Phase,* emotions fluctuate like a roller coaster. One minute you feel strong, as if you are finally gaining control over your emotions. The next minute, you feel as if you are spiraling downward. When I experienced this, small decisions like choosing what to eat or wear became overwhelming. Symptoms of emotional dysregulation can include:

- Abrupt or unexpected mood shifts
- Crying without knowing why
- An inability to calm down or difficulty soothing yourself
- Intense or disproportionate emotional reactions that are hard to control
- Feeling easily distressed or overwhelmed by your emotions
- Difficulty coping with stress
- Impulsive behavior without reflection or regard for consequences
- Being quick to take offense, outbursts of anger
- Substance misuse
- Suicidal thoughts[2] **NOTE—If you are having suicidal thoughts, please dial 988 to reach the Get Help-988 Lifeline (USA) or go to your nearest emergency room.**

In my *Storm Phase,* I felt so many emotions - disbelief, confusion, sadness, anger—and at times I even felt devoid of emotion, with a numbness that exceeded my understanding. It was baffling that my body could contain the sheer magnitude of these emotions without imploding.

Dr. Martin Seligman, innovative researcher and expert on learned optimism, suggests that we challenge our beliefs or emotions by examining their root causes.[3] A good way to manage intense emotions is to analyze each emotion individually. In my practice, I encourage clients to develop the skill of examining their emotions. Emotions can be amplified by unrelated or exaggerated fears. The challenge is to acknowledge the emotion, then respond in a healthy manner. When you feel scared, angry, or desperate, stop and take a deep breath. Feel and observe the emotion. Consider asking yourself:

- *What exactly am I feeling*
- *Is it fear-based*
- *Does this feeling contain truth*
- *Is it exaggerated*
- *Is it revealing something I have been avoiding, unwilling to face, or trying to ignore*

Before acting on an emotion, consider taking the time to share your feelings with someone you trust.

Teresa's Personal Experience

In my early thirties, I was trick-or-treating with my little ones when unexpectedly, I witnessed a traumatic event. Thankfully, my kids were too young and too busy trick-or-treating to notice. However, I couldn't get the frightening experience out of my head. In the past, autumn and Halloween had been my favorite time of year. Now, everything associated with Halloween and October filled me with dread as the event replayed in my mind. Finding daily tasks challenging, I felt broken and beyond repair—false beliefs and emotions were dominating my thoughts. I made an appointment with a counselor. Explaining what I had witnessed, I told her, "I can't eat. I can't

> *make decisions or concentrate. I feel lost and I don't know what to think."*
>
> *The counselor assured me, "You are normal! Everything you described is a typical response to trauma." That one counseling session gave me the clarity I needed. Understanding that my reactions were normal helped me heal. Over time, the experience became a distant memory—just a bump in the road. Recognizing my emotional responses were typical helped me identify and process my emotions.*

No matter the size of the tragic event or other types of trauma *Storms,* whether large or small, the emotional changes, though they feel overwhelming - are a good sign that you are responding in a normal or typical way to an atypical event. Developing the skill of questioning and examining our emotions helps us navigate through the *Storm Phase.* One of the best things to ever come out of psychological research is Dr. Martin Seligman's advice to dispute our thoughts by checking the accuracy of our reflexive beliefs. Beliefs may or may not be facts.[4] After trauma, it is easy to assume the worst about the future fueled by fear, anxiety, anger, shame, or guilt. Questioning these beliefs or disputes is a healthy way to manage the emotions that feel so overwhelming.

Identifying emotional changes is vital to surviving the *Storm Phase.* It is a triage of sorts. As you identify how you are coping, what has changed, and what is not working, you will understand that this is not a permanent way of life. I have witnessed this hundreds of times in my practice. You will recover and your emotions and life will return to a steady state - the sun will shine again.

Activities

1. Keep a log of your emotions in a notebook or on an electronic device.
2. If you have emotions of anger or frustration, find a safe activity to express the feeling, such as axe throwing, chopping wood, yelling in the woods, or a smash it / rage room in your community.
3. Make a habit of disputing your negative thoughts or feelings.

Sources

1 Crappy Childhood Fairy. (2022, March 15). *Trauma causes emotional dysregulation: Here's how to heal it* [Video]. YouTube. https://www.youtube.com/watch?v=4lZ2xTpNiqE

2 Dibdin, E. (2022, September 7). *How does PTSD lead to emotional dysregulation?* Psych Central. https://psychcentral.com/ptsd/affect-dysregulation-and-c-ptsd

3 Seligman, M.(1991). *Learned optimism*, p.222. Alfred A. Knopf, New York.

4 Seligman, M.(1991). *Learned optimism*, p.219-21. Alfred A. Knopf, New York.

CHAPTER 8

SPIRITUAL IMPACT

The Higher Journey

The journey inward is the journey outward.

— Adapted from Elizabeth O'Conner

One seldom acknowledged aspect of trauma is the spiritual impact experienced during the *Storm Phase.* My spiritual strength and foundation took a direct hit, causing profound confusion about my place in the world and my purpose.

Spirituality can refer to organized religion, cultural or traditional faith, personal beliefs, inner peace, connecting with the universe, being one with nature, astrology, a higher presence, or karma. For many, faith and spirituality form the foundation of an individual's identity, values and coping strategies. A traumatic experience can shake that framework, leading to increased stress and altered coping skills. We've all seen destruction after a storm. Regaining spiritual strength, stability, and equilibrium is a gradual process that requires patience.

As a woman of Christian faith, my belief system is part of my personal framework. As with many who experience trauma, I found myself questioning my identity: "Who am I? What is my purpose? Have I done something wrong to have been given this trial? How can I forgive? Is there a higher meaning to life?" Some may even ask difficult questions: "Has God forsaken me? Is the universe against me? What did I do to deserve this?"

The trauma *Storm Phase* can cause an individual to question their entire belief system as they try to make sense of life events and reconstruct how they approach the future. It can initiate or contribute to an existential crisis. To me, it was as if my deepest thoughts and feelings had a light shined on the innermost parts of my soul, exposing all my vulnerabilities while I searched for new understanding, meaning, and direction.

The destruction of a trauma leaves us to sort through and clean up our spiritual framework. I think of it as watching a majestic pine tree, a landmark for generations, give way and topple from a destructive windstorm. The tree that once protected us with its shade and shaped our landscape as a recognizable landmark is now gone. We can replant, but the shade and protection take time to develop. Trauma *Storms* can strip away the shade, the landmarks and protection our faith provided, leaving us feeling vulnerable and exposed, causing us to reexamine our belief system. We can rebuild, but like the landscape after losing a tree, it will look different.

The *National Institutes of Health* points out that "religious and spiritual cognitions should be considered in the context of trauma, because religious beliefs comprise a substantial part of many people's global meaning system and therefore inform their coping response."[1] Faith often shapes our coping strategies. I had to re-examine my faith and spirituality. This was significant for me as I had always been confident in my spiritual framework, and I never expected to question it.

I had to navigate many complex questions which started from my basic beliefs about myself, my purpose, and my life's path. Through this process, I chose to continue the spiritual path I was on before my traumatic experience. While some of the changes I experienced were difficult, my spiritual path offered new insights and provided opportunities to take greater ownership of my faith. I was able to ground again in my belief that I am a daughter of God, that I have a purpose on Earth specific to me, that I have a Heavenly Father I can pray to, and that Jesus Christ can make up the difference after my best efforts. Within the construct of these beliefs, I believe that hard things happen in this life, our personal agency cannot be taken away, and neither can the agency of others be removed, even when they cause pain.

Each of us will settle on different paths of spirituality on which to build our framework, all with the goal of finding peace and joy. Studies have shown that faith enhances health and recovery through mind-body-spirit healing in diverse cultural and religious beliefs.[2] Within these frameworks, we will find coping skills that will assist us in our healing. One of the greatest coping skills that helps me during my healing process is relying on prayer. Your framework will have coping skills too, so I encourage you to find them so they can bring you strength.

Activities

1. What has been the most important spiritual framework you have identified with in the past and how did it contribute positively to your life?
2. What part of your spiritual journey feels broken and needs to be rebuilt?
3. Are there new spiritual paths you would like to explore, change or strengthen?

Sources

1 Wortmann, J. H., Park, C. L., & Edmondson, D. (2011). Trauma and PTSD symptoms: Does spiritual struggle mediate the link? *Psychological Trauma Theory Research Practice and Policy, 3*(4), 442–452. https://doi.org/10.1037/a0021413

2 Grim, B. J., & Grim, M. E. (2019). Belief, Behavior, and Belonging: How Faith is Indispensable in Preventing and Recovering from Substance Abuse. *Journal of Religion and Health, 58*(5), 1713–1750. https://doi.org/10.1007/s10943-019-00876-w

CHAPTER 9

FEAR

Screaming Like the Passengers in His Car

I learned that courage was not the absence of fear, but the triumph over it.

— Nelson Mandela

There is an old joke that has been made into t-shirts and refrigerator magnets: "When I am old, I want to die like my grandfather who passed peacefully in his sleep, not screaming like the passengers in his car." While this joke is good for a laugh, it highlights how fear can make us feel like helpless passengers in our own lives. Trauma ignites fear and during my *Storm Phase* of trauma, fear became my most consuming emotion. In the eye of the *Storm,* we battle not only the trauma itself and the wounds it leaves behind but also the layers of heightened fears—both rational and irrational, that emerge in its wake.[1]

Loss of the Internal Monologue[2]

Heightened fears shake our confidence and disrupt our internal monologue, making it harder to solve problems and process decisions. Without our internal monologue to guide us, fear can push us back into the passenger seat. Responding in fear can complicate the ability to meet our basic needs including food, shelter, health, and employment. Trauma forces us to reframe certain aspects of our lives. Simple decisions that once felt automatic may now require structured reminders or checklists and significantly more time, energy, and effort. The compounding losses of trauma can cascade into other losses that can strip away independence, leading to greater instability, heightening fears, replacing clarity with a state of constant uncertainty. This loss of clarity can lead survivors to question their very identity, as one person often expressed; "I don't know who I am." She was not in the driver's seat. Fear squashed her internal dialogue, causing her to forget the confidence she once had in herself and her ability to solve problems.

Hyperarousal

After a significant traumatic event, the body can be locked in a state of hyperarousal. This state signals your brain to say, "I need to protect myself and keep myself emotionally and physically safe." During the *Storm* and *Clearing Phases* of my trauma experience, thoughts of safety became a primary governing emotion. Having been resilient and generally not fearful in the past, this state of hyperarousal triggered recollections of past experiences, clustered flashbacks that merged with the present, and together, these amplified my emotions.

Fear and hyperarousal do not always begin immediately after a traumatic experience. It can take days, weeks, or even months before the elements of hyperarousal kick in. Heightened fear reactions drain energy from essential processes such as sleeping, eating, socializing, and working. Anyone going through this may feel as if their ability to control even small things is weakened. Daily life may feel more challenging, exhausting, and overwhelming. Even though it is difficult, trust the process and continue to put one foot in front of the other. While the body and mind may feel overwhelmed, the path to healing requires trust in one's own ability to move into the driver's seat and move forward. It is difficult to feel as if you can trust your emotions and feelings. However, you've made good decisions in the past, and although it may require more thought, energy, and effort, you can continue to make good decisions.

Addressing Fears

Confronting fears will help rebuild confidence and is a positive step toward better decision making. Thoughts such as I will never get through this, I don't have enough resources, I can never make it on my own are thoughts that come out of fear. "Being afraid, is not the same as being in danger."[3] When working with clients on triggers or emotional responses, I often ask, "What is your fear?" Their answers lead to deeper discussions, helping uncover the origin of their fear while challenging inaccurate or negative beliefs along the way and identifying facts, new truths and realities.[4] Fear is a powerful hijacker of our story and emotions, stealing our sense of identity and causing us to believe we aren't smart enough, unworthy of happiness, or incapable of ever having a safe and harmonious life. These are all distortions of reality.

Fear, when based on truth, can serve as a protective emotion. It is true that fire burns, so we teach young children to be cautious and avoid it—this is a healthy, protective fear. Genuine, healthy fear can motivate us to make swift changes for a safer future. Learning and discovering the truth about trauma-induced fears can give us clarity. It helps restore confidence! Identifying the difference between healthy fears and irrational or exaggerated fears is another way to move from the backseat to the driver's seat. The goal is to identify the root cause of fear, preventing further limitations or emotional impairments. Developing the skill of asking questions to challenge fearful thoughts takes time and practice and leads to solutions, deeper understanding, and personal growth.[5]

Fear can cause us to focus on worst-case scenarios. Examining the worst-case scenarios is a healthy response and part of practical risk assessment and problem solving. After a traumatic event, it is wise to re-examine your risk exposure and situational triggers. Along with that, it is prudent to develop safety plans in case of a new crisis arising. These are excellent ways to protect yourself and reduce fear.[6] The problem arises when fear becomes the sole focus, leaving us stuck in a panic, unable to pull ourselves back to a realistic view of the situation and our capabilities. Fear can distort reality and create unnecessary obstacles, making life harder than it needs to be.

Fear is such a problem in our society that over 2,500 years ago, ancient Chinese philosopher and founder of Taoism Lao Tzu taught, "There is no illusion greater than fear."[7] Fear, fueled by our perceived vulnerabilities, can distort our perception of reality, leading to unnecessary suffering. In a trauma *Storm,* fear can manifest as overwhelming or paralyzing questions in our minds.

- *What if I am not strong enough to face this illness*
- *How do I go on by myself*
- *How will I take care of my children*
- *What if I never feel safe*
- *What happens if I am all alone in the world*
- *What if no one ever loves me*
- *How will I pay my rent*
- *Why am I not enough*
- *Why do I feel so stupid*
- *What if I fail*
- *Why am I so impatient*

These questions can be related to physical, emotional, or spiritual safety. Trauma can leave us terrified of being abandoned, judged, unloved, betrayed, weak, or unable to provide financially.

Sorting Things Out

The motto of my company, Lucent Counseling and Consulting, is "*Clarity Creates Confidence.*" Spending the time, energy, and effort to clarify our thoughts helps defeat fear, doubt, and insecurity and restore an authentic inner monologue. Seeking clarity is similar to doing a puzzle by turning puzzle pieces upright and then sorting them by edges, shapes, and colors to create organization out of chaos. It has been said that the opposite of fear is knowledge and understanding. Discovering new insights or understandings begins with curiosity, leading to investigation, which then leads to learning and ultimately gaining clarity.

Like a puzzle, connecting the pieces of trauma together form a clearer picture of fear's origin. Allowing us to find ways to define, address, and resolve the fear. Egyptian poet Naguib Mahfouz (1911-2006) wrote, "Fear does not prevent death. It prevents life."[8] Identifying the

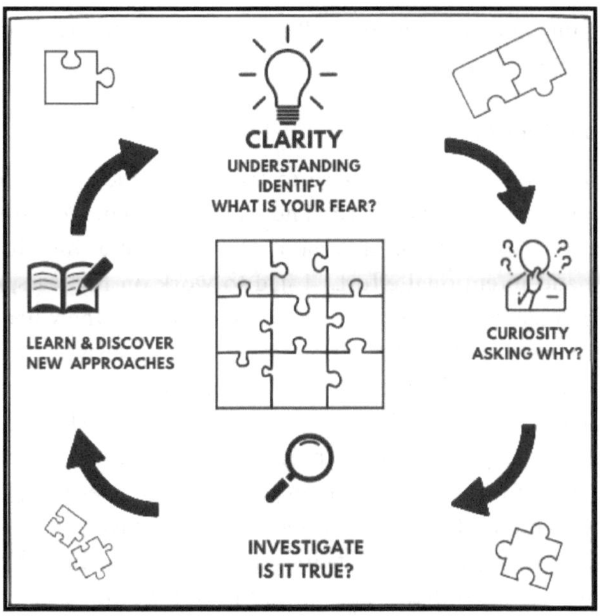

root of fear helps us to face, address, and ultimately confront the fear, which helps us improve the overall quality of life.

Relying upon a car analogy with my clients, I will ask, "Are you in the front seat driving your car?" The car represents their life and story. If they reply that they see themselves in the passenger seat or in the back seat screaming in fear, we have some work to do by asking about their fear and why they feel the way they do. We need to determine whether the fear is based in truth and what can be done next. With every difficult trauma, especially during the *Storm* and *Clearing Phase,* there will be days when we feel as if we are sitting in the backseat screaming!

Running from our fears, only make them seem larger and scarier. Confronting fear unlocks strength, courage, and confidence. Whether you decide to face the fear head on, talk about your fears with a friend or counselor, or create a plan on how to approach something that scares you, you can conquer fear. No one should be forced to live in permanent fear, but it requires us to face those fears, essentially moving from the back seat and sitting up front in the driver's seat. We decide where we are going, and how fast we will get there. Turn the key, step on the accelerator. Move forward.

Triumph Over Fear

While fear is a natural response to trauma, by facing our fears, we move from uncertainty to clarity and fear can be removed. Again, like most work in overcoming trauma, it is one step at a time. It requires patience and intentional effort. I had to work on my fears, one at a time. The majority of the time I find myself behind the wheel, sitting in the driver's seat of my metaphorical car—which feels empowering! I still have moments when fear takes over, and I figuratively slip into the back seat and scream a little. That is when I return to asking questions, investigating my fears, determining what is true, and resuming my journey from the driver's seat. Every instance we question a fear represents moving back into the driver's seat. As I have witnessed brave clients figuratively leave their fears behind and move into the driver's seat, I am reminded that we each have power within us to overcome fear and reclaim our lives rather than screaming like the other passengers in the car.

Activities

1. Talk to someone you trust about one of your fears.
2. Brainstorm ways you could face that fear.
3. Make an intentional plan to face one of your fears.

Sources

1 Brown, H. B. (1988). *An abundant life: The Memoirs of Hugh B. Brown* (E. Firmage, Ed.).

2 Internal dialogue is referred to as inner monologue or internal dialogue or a combination of either term.

3 TEDx Talks. (2014, June 16). How to make stress your friend | Kelly McGonigal | TEDxSanFrancisco [Video]. YouTube. https://www.youtube.com/watch?v=jryCoo0BrRk

4 Seligman, M. E. P. (1991). *Learned optimism.* Knopf.

5 Brodsky, J. (2021, November 22). Why questioning is the ultimate learning skill. *Forbes.* https://www.forbes.com/sites/juliabrodsky/2021/12/29/why-questioning-is-the-ultimate-learning-sMiciano, M. T. (2024, November 21). *Understanding inner monologue: examples of internal dialogue and life without it.* Narra Counselling & Consulting. https://www.narracounselling.com/blogs/understanding-inner-monologue

6 Zhang, Y. (2024, November 29). *What could go wrong? | The value of worst-case scenario planning.* https://www.controlrisks.com/our-thinking/insights/the-value-of-worst-case-scenario-planning

7 *BK: Tao: There is no greater illusion than fear — Out Of Suffering.* (n.d.). Out of Suffering. https://www.outofsuffering.com/bk-tao-there-is-no-greater-illusion-than-fear

8 Mairi. (2022, January 6). *Reflections on Fear - Change is Always Possible.* Change Is Always Possible. https://changeisalwayspossible.com/reflections-on-fear/

CHAPTER 10

PTSD OR CPTSD

Battle Fatigue

There isn't a formula that you can insert
yourself into to get from horror to healed.
Be patient. Take up space. Let your journey be the balm.

— Dawn Serra

During the *Storm Phase* of a traumatic experience, it is normal to experience sleep disruptions, feel disoriented, or relive difficult memories. In time, these symptoms should improve. However, if they persist beyond six to eight weeks, worsen, become disruptive, or they continue to resurface years later, this may indicate post-traumatic stress disorder (PTSD) or complex PTSD (CPTSD).

Like many others who are diagnosed with PTSD, I never imagined that PTSD recovery would become part of my journey. PTSD can develop months or even years after a traumatic event and may involve nightmares, intrusive memories, re-experiencing the trauma, negative thoughts, sleeping difficulties, being easily startled, challenges with concentration, or avoiding places, thoughts, or triggers connected to a traumatic event.[1] PTSD is not a sign of weakness, it is a condition that can develop after a difficult experience that becomes stuck in your mind.

One of my PTSD symptoms is heightened sensitivity to sound. Unexpected noises make me jump and send shock throughout my body. I also began to have nightmares and restless sleep, unlike my usual patterns. Interrupted sleep and other symptoms coincided with days that I experienced trauma triggers. When PTSD symptoms first appeared, they added to the emotional heaviness of what I was already carrying.

I felt discouraged, knowing there were yet more challenges to face. I could not help but worry whether my mind would ever return to its normal clarity.

With time though, the symptoms have lessened, and my brain is healing, just as I have seen in many of my clients. Our brains have the capacity to overcome and heal.[2] I am living proof of the healing process. I want to assure you there are interventions to help reduce the symptoms and reactions, and life will get better.

How PTSD Occurs

The prefrontal cortex area of the human brain is responsible for regulating emotions, solving problems, sorting multiple streams of information, planning, and making decisions.[3] The small, almond-shaped amygdala, located in the brain's center, is responsible for alerting us to danger. When exposed to a traumatic or catastrophic event, these two systems—the prefrontal cortex and the amygdala—get stuck in a loop, becoming dysregulated. Rather than protecting us from danger, the amygdala signals that danger is *everywhere,* placing the rest of your body, including your hormones, into an unnecessary, constant alarm mode. The constant state of alert can make it difficult to live a normal, healthy life without some help or intervention. Some scientists consider PTSD a brain injury.[4]

PTSD Facts

- *PTSD can affect individuals who have experienced or witnessed any type of trauma, such as an automobile accident, major medical event, an assault, the loss of a family member or close companion, or any other traumatic event*
- *PTSD is not a sign of weakness or a character flaw*
- *Women develop PTSD somewhat more frequently than men*[5]

Effective Treatment Options

Living with the effects of PTSD can feel discouraging; however, specific clinical therapies have proven effective.[6] More recent studies by Shrader and Ross from *Veteran Affairs (VA)* show that therapies such as Cognitive Processing Therapy (CPT), Prolonged Exposure Therapy (PE), and Eye-Movement Desensitization and Reprocessing (EMDR) are among the most effective treatment options.[7] More in-depth information about these and other treatment modalities will be discussed in the *Clearing* section of this book. No one should be condemned to live the rest of their lives with PTSD as there are effective, safe, and accessible treatments available.

If you are dealing with what you suspect is PTSD, please seek medical intervention and therapy as soon as possible. The sooner you seek treatment—the sooner you can access effective tools to reduce symptoms related to PTSD.[8]

Authors' Note: CPTSD and PTSD are categorized and recognized differently by the World Health Organization (WHO) and the American Psychiatric Association (APA). The information provided in this book is intended for general public use and should not be construed as a substitute for professional diagnosis or treatment. It is important to note that some professional organizations may hold differing opinions. This book aims to present the available information objectively, without advocating for or against any particular perspective.

Activities

1. If you feel you have PTSD, write down the symptoms in order to share with a medical provider or mental health therapist.
2. Draw a picture that visually explains your feelings and symptoms.
3. Draw a picture of what you would like your feelings and symptoms to feel like after recovery.

Sources

1 The Recovery Village. (2021, February 8). *The science and biology of PTSD – PTSD UK*. https://www.ptsduk.org/what-is-ptsd/the-science-and-biology-of-ptsd/

2 Bennett, H. (2023, July 12). *Neuroplasticity: A neurologist explains how the brain recovers from injury*. BBC Science Focus Magazine. https://www.sciencefocus.com/the-human-body/can-brain-heal-itself

3 Bandoim, L. (2023, September 14). *The anatomy of the prefrontal cortex*. Verywell Health. https://www.verywellhealth.com/prefrontal-cortex-5220699

4 *The science and biology of PTSD – PTSD UK*. (n.d.). https://www.ptsduk.org/what-is-ptsd/the-science-and-biology-of-ptsd/

5 *How trauma affects the body: Understanding the impact*. (2024b, September 17). COPE Psychology Center. https://copepsychology.com/how-trauma-affects-the-body/

6 Mendes, D. D., Mello, M. F., Ventura, P., De Medeiros Passarela, C., & De Jesus Mari, J. (2008). A Systematic Review on the Effectiveness of Cognitive Behavioral therapy for Posttraumatic Stress Disorder. *The International Journal of Psychiatry in Medicine, 38*(3), 241–259. https://doi.org/10.2190/pm.38.3.b

7 Schrader, C., & Ross, A. (2021b, December 1). *A review of PTSD and current treatment strategies*. https://pmc.ncbi.nlm.nih.gov/articles/PMC8672952/

8 *VA.gov | Veterans Affairs*. (n.d.-e). https://www.ptsd.va.gov/gethelp/index.asp

CHAPTER 11

DEPRESSION

Inside the Darkness

I saw the world in black and white instead of the vibrant colors and shades I knew existed.

— Katie McGarry

If you or a loved one are struggling with depression, contact the Substance Abuse and Mental Health Services Administration (SAMHSA) National Helpline at ***1-800-662-4357*** *for information on support and treatment facilities in your area or dial* ***988*** *for the Suicide and Crisis Lifeline.*

If this is your first experience with depression, regardless of the type of depression you have been diagnosed with, it can feel a lot like a vacuum—it sucks. The complex variables of trauma—stress, genetics, illness, hormones, and even the time of year—can trigger a depressive disorder. It can arise anytime, interfering with the function of daily life.[1]

Some individuals will battle depression their whole lives, while others from similar backgrounds and circumstances may only experience depression infrequently or not at all. Although women are twice as likely as men to suffer from depression, depression can hit anyone anytime and for almost any reason. Stress and trauma can be catalysts for the onset of depression. Regardless of financial circumstance, status, affluence, achievements or expertise, no one is immune to depression. When life seems too hard or too overwhelming, seeking help is a good idea.[2] No matter the type of depression or how long you have been working through it, you are not alone. If you have been suffering from depressive symptoms for more than two weeks, please seek medical intervention.

Considering my family history of depression combined with a history of childhood trauma, it is surprising I haven't experienced more depressive episodes throughout my life. Before my traumatic experience, I had only experienced two depressive episodes—one as a result of grief, which is covered in the section on grief, and another likely caused by Seasonal Affective Disorder. In both cases, I was able to work through them successfully. My third depressive episode was a direct result of my traumatic experience. As this book reflects my journey, I feel pressed to share that writing about depression is one of the hardest portions of this book. As a trauma therapist, I help others, yet even with all my skills, practice, and knowledge, I experienced clinical depression for more than a year after my traumatic experience.

Depression lasts longer and is more persistent than a general feeling of disappointment, sadness, or worry. It can feel like a sinkhole of suffering or a dark abyss that is too deep to climb out of. Although depression comes in different forms and models, it consistently interferes with perspective, emotions, activities, eating and sleeping patterns and other aspects of life. When life feels impossible, unbearably heavy, or overwhelming, that is depression. Depression looks a little different for everyone who experiences it. Some lose their appetite, while others overeat. Some struggle with insomnia, while others can't get out of bed. Some become hypersensitive to rejection or criticism, while others feel numb and indifferent. Common types of depression include:

- Major Depressive Disorder (Clinical Depression)
- Atypical Depression
- Persistent Depressive Disorder (Chronic Depression)

- Bipolar Disorder (Manic/Depressive)
- Postpartum Depression
- Premenstrual Dysphoric Disorder
- Seasonal Affective Disorder (Lack of Sunlight)[3]

There is no single solution for depression, but identifying the type of depression, or the root of the depression, is the beginning step to recovery.[4]

Symptoms of Depression

Mayo Clinic expert Craig Sawchuk, Ph.D., L.P. lists symptoms of major depressive disorder:

- Feelings of sadness, tearfulness, emptiness, or hopelessness
- Angry outbursts, irritability, or frustration, even over small matters
- Loss of interest or pleasure in most or all normal activities, such as sex, hobbies, or sports
- Sleep disturbances, including insomnia or sleeping too much
- Tiredness and lack of energy, so even small tasks take extra effort
- Reduced appetite and weight loss or increased cravings for food and weight gain
- Anxiety, agitation, or restlessness
- Slowed thinking, speaking, or body movements
- Feelings of worthlessness or guilt, fixating on past failures, or self-blame
- Trouble thinking, concentrating, making decisions, and remembering things
- Frequent or recurrent thoughts of death, suicidal thoughts, or suicide attempts
- Unexplained physical problems, such as back pain or headaches[5]

Depression Factors

While almost everyone experiences stressful events, not everyone develops depression. According to cognitive psychologists, a key factor in developing depression is the distress caused when deeply held beliefs or expectations about how the world should work, or when reality contradicts our expectations are unmet. This kind of disappointment, or jarring disillusionment can feel like an unexpected topple over a cliff's edge, triggering emotional distress and depression. Another contributing factor to developing depression is early or profound loss, particularly in women who were abused as children. One risk factor we do have some control over is vitamin D deficiency. Dr. James Greenbalt warns that vitamin D deficiency is an "underlying biochemical risk factor" for depression, suicide, and anxiety. Researchers are discovering connections between insufficient vitamin D and other neuroprotective agents. The number of people who suffer from insufficient vitamin D worldwide is alarming. Vitamin D deficiency or a host of other medical conditions can contribute to depression.[6] Consult licensed medical providers if you have any medical concerns.

For many individuals, it is normal to experience episodes of depression, including situational depression, which can occur after a stressful or sad event. Some professionals may classify it as an adjustment disorder with depressed mood or reactive depression. Scenarios that could contribute to situational depression may include a breakup, work or school-related difficulties, a death, a medical diagnosis, financial strain, or any other stressful life event that makes you feel overwhelmed, stressed, or sad. Individual stress responses vary based on multiple factors including genetic makeup, circumstances, previous experiences, and the length or type of stress. Combining these factors can result in any number of cascading physiological responses that can result in depression.[7]

Postpartum Depression

In the miraculous birth of a child, the last thing any mother expects is postpartum depression. As humans, we naturally look for the best outcomes. Television and media portrayals of birth can often make it seem effortless and uneventful. Women will sometimes mention having the "baby blues," which is a short-term readjustment of the mother's hormones after delivery. Postpartum depression is more intense and lasts longer than the baby blues. It can stem from a traumatic birth, a difficult pregnancy, compromised health of the newborn, or follow a completely normal, healthy delivery.

Postpartum depression is debilitating and happens more frequently than expected. If left untreated, it can negatively impact mother-infant attachment, cause deeper and longer-lasting mental and psychological disorders for the mother, and be a detriment to the entire family.[8] It is important to be genuine with trusted medical professionals and candid when completing mental health screening assessments so you can receive proper care.

Seasonal Affective Disorder (SAD)

About twenty years ago, my first experience with depression came when a military assignment took my family to a small, isolated peninsula 33 miles above the Arctic Circle called Kotzebue, Alaska. It was a frontier experience, especially as we were bringing four children aged four to eleven to what felt like—and quite literally was—the end of the earth.

Less than 25 square miles in size, the only way into or out of the isolated Kotzebue peninsula is a pricey plane ride. Trading my van, sun, open highways, and four distinct seasons for snow machines and freezing temperatures, along with being confined to this small peninsula and the typical arctic darkness and extreme weather that kept us inside most of the year, all combined to pave the way for some challenging times. Some individuals love this type of adventure, but it was hard for me. I felt trapped, frozen, and isolated while trying to create a happy experience for my children, have a good attitude, and embrace our adventure.

During the second year of the assignment, I fell into a severe depression. Depression, much like trauma, distorts our sense of time, making our assignment in Kotzebue feel much longer than two years.

Trying to counter the cloud over my head, Matchbox 20's 2002 hit "Unwell" became a favorite song I played on repeat. Lead singer Rob Thomas' lyrics hit home and have become an anthem for those living with depression and anxiety.[9] I knew that even though I didn't feel like myself, this experience was temporary and the brighter, happier side of me would appear again after I moved away from the Arctic, but in the meantime, life felt difficult! Inupiat women of the village joked about naming me "white girl who doesn't like to go outside." Thankfully, I ended up with the name 'Aqpik,' which means sweet and tangy berry. I liked that better!

Major Depressive Disorder

In this book, each chapter typically begins with something from my traumatic experience, but as this is the most difficult part to discuss, I saved it until the end of this section. I feel an obligation to be as gentle as possible with this section. If you are experiencing depression, *please get help*. Talk to someone you trust or have seen go through difficult things, use the phone numbers listed at the beginning of this chapter, or call your doctor. Don't wait another moment. All you have to say is, "I need help. I am not okay."

After my traumatic experience, the depression and despair, or sinkhole of suffering, took root. This part of my journey is where I had to intentionally fight against the darkness that engulfed me and fight for peace and joy. I usually have an innate ability to be optimistic and take a stressful event head-on, but during my trauma, the combination and sheer amount of stressors knocked me off my feet and brought me down the path of severe depression for well over a year.

Without any plans to act, I did have moments where living seemed too difficult, giving rise to thoughts of not wanting to live. Depression buried me in a dark hole. It was difficult to feel happiness. I could not see light or hope. The darkness that overwhelmed me felt insurmountable. I was never technically suicidal, having no plans to take my life as I didn't want to die, but living felt so painful. Although depressed, I had the capacity to know I did not want and would not want my loved ones—especially my children—to be burdened with the type of pain that comes from a life coming to an end. More importantly, I wanted to experience their lives and be present with them. The hardest part of living with depression is convincing yourself that life will not always feel so painful. And yet, when you are suffering so deeply, the pain is inescapable, requiring a great deal of mental and physical energy to pull out of the dark abyss. During this time, I relied on family and friends, sought professional medical help and counsel from religious advisors. It was pervasive; it took over a year to find joy and happiness regularly.

Climbing Out of Depression

Regrettably, depression does not lift like an airplane. You can't turn on the engine, pull up the rudder, and fly up and out of depression. Climbing out of depression is like climbing up and out of a deep pit. At the halfway mark, the perspective of the work required can appear as if you are making very little progress, discounting all the work you've done to get where you are. Overshadowed by the challenge in front of you, it is easy to be tempted to give up or let go and fall to the bottom. Author Brad Wilcox illustrates the nature of change by saying, "Realizing that change is a process, [we] would never get angry at a seed for not being a flower or expect a sculptor to transform a block of marble into a masterpiece overnight."[10] Expecting change to be easy, swift, or inconsequential is not realistic.

In addition to professional help and reliance on friends and family, to help counterbalance the constant pull of the dark abyss I would purposely say aloud to myself, "Kelli, look around. There are so many amazing people in your life, so many opportunities still to be grasped, so many people still to meet, and so much of the world still to explore. Your life is so much more than this moment. Don't let trauma steal that from you."

I intentionally thought about the beautiful things in my world. I am privileged to live next to gorgeous and breathtaking mountains that remind me of the amazing world we live in. At night, I would gaze at the stars and imagine all that exists that I still haven't explored. Having recovered from prior depressive episodes I had experienced, along with witnessing my clients' recovery, I knew eventually I would find light and purpose again in my life.

Depression, along with all the other trauma responses, can cause us to focus on a sliver of life that feels overwhelming and out of control or that makes us feel betrayed, lost, hopeless, and heartbroken. It creates a tunnel vision where only darkness is visible and we feel helpless. Depression, like anxiety, can steal our sense of reality, convincing us that our lives are consumed by hopeless despair, even though there is still much that is good and right. It can distort our view of the future, leading us to believe there's nothing to look forward to when there are still wonderful people and experiences ahead. Depression can rob us of hope, when, in fact, there is much to hope for.

Silver Linings

While every type of depression is different, you can still experience moments of happiness during clinical depression. I had times of joy and silver linings during my Arctic adventure, including making lifelong friends, experiencing a new culture, and witnessing breathtaking National Geographic types of encounters. I saw a part of the world many people don't, took part in a different culture, and developed new skills. This time in our family's history gave us a unique bond, and my kids and I still talk about our Arctic adventures and how we survived.

Holocaust survivor Corrie ten Boom's life story is one of triumph over tragedy that reflects how I feel about depression.[11] The challenges and difficulties we face are interwoven with silver and golden threads. This concept is beautifully portrayed in the following poem, which Corrie ten Boom frequently shared. Even those who embrace different forms of spirituality can find wisdom in these words and understand that trauma can lead to personal growth and silver linings.

"The Weaver" by Grant Colfax Tullar

My life is but a weaving
Between my God and me.
I cannot choose the colors
He weaveth steadily.

Oft' times He weaveth sorrow;
And I in foolish pride
Forget He sees the upper
And I the underside.

Not 'til the loom is silent
And the shuttles cease to fly
Will God unroll the canvas
And reveal the reason why.

The dark threads are as needful
In the weaver's skillful hand
As the threads of gold and silver
In the pattern He has planned.

He knows, He loves, He cares;
Nothing this truth can dim.
He gives the very best to those
Who leave the choice to Him.[12]

Finally, thank you for walking with me as you go through the *Trauma Impact Phases.* What lies ahead may feel steep, but I promise the sun will start peeking through the shadows. As I intentionally worked on transforming trauma into hope and healing, with time, resources, and therapy the depression has resolved. Yours can too. We were created to be resilient and to do extraordinary things. You've already done extraordinary things by coming this far with me.

In time, you will notice the sun coming out again. Confidence will return, and glorious normality will begin to fill your days. The future is bright. Please hold on as there are resources available to reduce depressive symptoms. Don't give up hope! Healing, hope, joy, and empowerment are ahead.

Activities

1. What symptoms do you have that are associated with depression?
2. If the symptoms have persisted, identify a plan to seek treatment through your medical doctor and mental health therapist.
3. Write down or draw how you envision your life once your depressive symptoms decrease.

Sources

1 Gans, MD, S. (Ed.). (2023, December 7). *Depression: Overview and more.* Verywell Mind. https://www.verywellmind.com/depression-4157261

2 Siqueland, L., (2021, February 17). *How to know when to seek therapy.* Anxiety and Depression Association of America, ADAA. Retrieved January 6, 2025, from https://adaa.org/learn-from-us/from-the-experts/blog-posts/consumer/how-know-when-seek-therapy

3 Schimelpfening, N. (2023b, June 16). 7 common types of depression. *Verywell Mind.* https://www.verywellmind.com/common-types-of-depression-1067313

4 Edwards, S. (2019, February 2). *Finding the root cause of depression for proper diagnosis and treatment | Dr. Sarah Edwards, PhD, LCSW.* Dr. Sarah Edwards, PhD, LCSW | Counseling Adults Teens Children Couples. https://www.drsarahedwards.com/finding-the-root-cause-of-depression-for-proper-diagnosis-and-treatment/

5 Sawchuk, C., Ph. D. ,L. P. ,. (n.d.). *Depression (major depressive disorder) - Symptoms and causes.* Mayo Clinic. https://www.mayoclinic.org/diseases-conditions/depression/symptoms-causes/syc-20356007Schimelpfening, N. (2023, June 16). 7 common types of depression. *Verywell Mind.* https://www.verywellmind.com/common-types-of-depression-1067313

6 Greenblatt, J. M., MD. (2024, October 9). Mental Health in the Sun: The role of Vitamin D deficiency in Mental illness. *Psychiatric Times.* https://www.psychiatrictimes.com/view/mental-health-in-the-sun-the-role-of-vitamin-d-deficiency-in-mental-illness

7 Harvard Health. (2022, January 10). *How genes and life events affect mood and depression.* https://www.health.harvard.edu/depression/how-genes-and-life-events-affect-mood-and-depression

8 Hunker, D. F., Patrick, T. E., Albrecht, S. A., & Wisner, K. L. (2009). Is difficult childbirth related to postpartum maternal outcomes in the early postpartum period? *Archives of Women S Mental Health, 12*(4), 211–219. https://doi.org/10.1007/s00737-009-0068-3

9 Chen, H., & Chen, H. (2024, August 9). *Hear us out: Matchbox Twenty's 'Unwell' is more relevant than ever.* VICE. https://www.vice.com/en/article/matchbox-twenty-unwell-2003-mental-health-anxiety-nostalgia/

10 LDS Quotations, & Wilcox, B. (n.d.). *Quotes by Brad Wilcox | Page 2 of 2 | LDS Quotations.* LDS Quotations. https://ldsquotations.com/author/brad-wilcox/page/2/

11 Backhouse, H. C. (1992). *Corrie ten boom: Faith Triumphs.*

12 The Revival Channel. (2023, March 30). *Corrie Ten Boom's Favorite Poem - My Life is Like a Weaving* [Video]. YouTube. https://www.youtube.com/watch?v=kbaM44fCDuc

CHAPTER 12

ANXIETY

My Anxiety Has Anxiety

Worry often gives a small thing a big shadow.

— Swedish Proverb

Before my trauma experience, I had never experienced panic attacks, although I had worked with many clients who had. Sharing our understanding of certain physical or emotional human experiences can be challenging until we have a similar experience. Through the years, clients have described their trauma *Storms*, saying "I felt like I was going to die. I couldn't breathe. My heart was pounding out of my chest. I was so restless, I couldn't move. I can't think straight, but my mind is racing." Other physical symptoms include sweating, freezing, or feeling exhausted with an inability to sleep. Trauma brings on extremes as the anxiety stimulates, or more accurately, overstimulates the body into panic.

After my first panic attack, I connected with my clients' experiences on a deeper level. My already deep sense of empathy has grown even stronger because I know exactly what they mean, and I would not wish the sense of impending doom and feeling out of sorts on anyone. Anxiety and panic attacks can feel very much like a straitjacket, trapping you in physical and emotional symptoms. Often when panic sets in, it triggers even more panic. After experiencing this multiple times, some clients and I chuckle at what seems like an absurdity: anxiety can arise because we feel anxious about the possibility of experiencing anxiety again. For anyone going through this, it can feel as if even their anxiety has anxiety!

After experiencing trauma firsthand, my understanding of anxiety completely changed. A certain level of anxiety has a positive role in our day-to-day lives to protect and motivate us; however, when it impacts our lives negatively, it is best to find ways to reduce the impact. After a trauma, anxiety can be acute, meaning it arises suddenly with great intensity, or chronic, meaning it is always present and must be managed regularly. Regardless of the type of anxiety, the goal remains the same: reduce the symptoms and feel more in control of the physical and emotional responses.

In my practice, a helpful analogy I use is that once you have been bitten by a dog, your body may always respond to dogs and be more alert, but you learn skills that will help you navigate the circumstance and change the anxiety response. Viktor Frankl, who lost most of his family during the Holocaust in concentration camps, taught that people can find meaning even in the worst circumstances. The goal is not to deny the pain, the anxiety, or the hardships, but to use those experiences to change our perspective and navigate stormy seas.[1] Triggers will exist after a trauma *Storm*. Anxiety cannot be wiped out, but it can be managed.

Through my trauma experience, the variety of unexpected anxiety responses became an opportunity to concentrate on new skills to reframe specific triggers. My previous boundaries and comfort zones had all shifted and the anxiety was on full blast. Normal experiences that had never caused anxiety before could now trigger an anxiety response such as intense fear, heart palpitations, and sheer panic. Tasks that had never been difficult were no longer easy. I describe it this way: the new normal feels anything but normal, no matter what I do.

Many who have experienced trauma *Storms* describe being triggered by sights, sounds, or smells associated with their trauma. Someone who has been in a car accident could be triggered by a similar car, the smell of gasoline, or the sound of a siren. Nausea, heart racing, fast breathing or pounding in the ears are some of the common warning signs from the sympathetic nervous system, signaling perceived danger. These symptoms can escalate into anxiety or a panic attack. As everyone who has experienced trauma knows, anxiety triggers are endless, and they can arise from an infinite number of causes. These triggers can be as simple as a silly TV show, lyrics from a song, a memory that rises from nowhere, a thought shared at church, the inflection or way something is said, a sound, motion, or object, a particular place, or even opportunities such as public speaking, which often brings a small amount of normal anxiety. Anxiety, while difficult, is a form of self-protection. It takes time and experience to retrain your mind that you are now okay and safe. Be patient and kind to yourself during your journey toward healing.

Our physical and emotional trauma responses are instinctive.[2] These instinctive responses can include fight, flight, freeze, or fawning as the human body works to protect itself.[3]

- **Fight** means to respond with physical or verbal aggression. Arguing, yelling, or physical aggression are forms of the natural fight response. Signs of a fight response can include:
    - Teeth grinding or jaw clenching
    - The impulse to hit, punch, kick, or slap
    - Extreme feelings of anger, or thoughts of harming someone, even yourself
    - Weeping or crying
    - Sharply staring at other people
    - A knot in the stomach, upset stomach, or even a burning feeling in the stomach
    - Attacking the perceived source of the danger
- **Flight** means protecting ourselves by evading, retreating, or fleeing from potential harm. Signs of a flight response can include:
    - Excessive physical activity or exercise
    - Twitching, feeling impatient or antsy, or constantly moving
    - Tingling or numbness in extremities

- Rapidly shifting gaze or dilated eyes

- **Freeze** means being paralyzed or unable to respond or escape a threat. Signs of a freeze response can include:
  - A ghostly, gray pallor or pale skin
  - A sense of foreboding, dread, or panic
  - A feeling of heaviness, stiffness, or cement-like legs
  - Loud, racing, or pounding heart
  - Being unable to move or make decisions
- **Fawn** means responding by intentionally pleasing others to maintain peace in a tense situation or avoiding conflict through submissive behavior. Signs of a fawning response can include:
  - Children becoming the parent figure to appease a struggling parent
  - Servant-like behaviors, including doing whatever is necessary to keep the peace and please another person in a familial, workplace, friendship, or other relationship
  - Forfeiture of boundaries, rights, and needs [4]

Activating the vagus nerve in our bodies can reset feelings of panic or anxiety. This nerve lowers blood pressure and can help counterbalance some of the symptoms of the Four Fs. Scientists discovered that cold water on your face activates the vagus nerve and reduces anxiety.[5] An ice pack on the neck, a cold burst of water after a shower, or soaking your hands or feet in cold or cool water are all ways to help reset the vagus nerve and calm anxiety. Throughout this book, there will be more information on specific tools to overcome anxiety and panic attacks. Some people need music, meditation, and laughter. Others find peace or calm through cleaning and organizing, or exercise. The idea is to experiment on yourself and find what helps you defeat panic. Trauma removes confidence and creates a black hole of self-doubt, inferiority, and insecurity. One step at a time, line upon line, you will be able to replace pieces of the darkness with light, hope, and healing. Recognizing anxiety and panic attacks as part of the damage was a large part of my survival through the *Storm Phase.* The time will come to repair the damage, but it is impossible to clean up while in the middle of a *Storm.* You would never step outside during a tornado, so be patient and wait for the *Storm* to pass.

Anxiety symptoms can be significantly reduced or resolved through the use of tools, intervention strategies, resources, and possibly medication. Like everything worth working for, overcoming anxiety takes time and effort. Eventually, the body will learn new patterns. It may feel like a slow and tedious process but hold onto hope and the knowledge that your body has the ability to learn new patterns and responses.

At times, certain trauma responses may provoke an anxiety response in my body, but my journey of healing has given me more control over the responses. Now, watching television and listening to music are less anxiety-provoking. Sitting in church now feels more peaceful and spiritually fulfilling. Giving speeches or appearing in public forums feels more manageable and I can organize my thoughts faster. My body isn't as reactive to sounds and motion. Having worked through the *Trauma Impact Phases,* I have been on both sides of trauma. I have accepted that some triggers may always be part of my life, but like scars that remain with you after a difficult accident, they also become signs of resilience and strength. Managing anxiety and panic attacks is practical and attainable. I have learned to manage my anxiety, and with time, patience and the right tools, you will too.

Activities

1. What symptoms have you recognized that are associated with anxiety?
2. Can you identify if you experience Fight, Flight, Freeze, or a Fawn response? If so, what does that look like?
3. How has anxiety held you back from an activity or goal? What would it take to allow you to participate in that activity or goal again?

Sources

1 Hartley, E. (2024, July 12). *7 lessons from Viktor Frankl that will help anyone who feels life has lost its meaning.* Global English Editing. https://geediting.com/7-lessons-from-viktor-frankl-that-will-help-anyone-who-feels-life-has-lost-its-meaning/

2 *The 4F's of trauma response: fight, flight, freeze, and fawn.* (2024, October). Therapy Trainings. Retrieved December 23, 2024, from https://www.therapytrainings.com/pages/blog/the-4-fs-of-trauma-response-fight-flight-freeze-and-fawn

3 Guy-Evans MSC, O. G. (2023, November 9). *Fight, flight, freeze, or fawn: How we respond to threats.* Simply Psychology. https://www.simplypsychology.org/fight-flight-freeze-fawn.html

4 Walker, P. (n.d.). *Codependency, trauma and the fawn response.* https://www.pete-walker.com/pdf/CodependencyTraumaFawnResponse.pdf

5 Mäkinen, T. M., Mäntysaari, M., Pääkkönen, T., Jokelainen, J., Palinkas, L. A., Hassi, J., Leppäluoto, J., Tahvanainen, K., & Rintamäki, H. (2008). *Autonomic nervous function during Whole-Body Cold exposure before and after cold acclimation.* Aviation Space and Environmental Medicine, 79(9), 875–882. https://doi.org/10.3357/asem.2235.2008

CHAPTER 13

GRIEF

The Generous Gift of Grief

Your grief path is yours alone, and no one else can walk it, and no one else can understand it.

— Terri Irwin

The Impact of Grief

The physical effects of grief, sorrow, and loss can take anyone by surprise. What is particularly striking is the physical intensity of grief, from deep muscle aches and tightness, to piercing headaches, anguished sobs, and the unrelenting flow of tears. In the deepest part of my grief, it felt as if I had shed millions of tears, more tears in one year than all my previous years combined. It was difficult to comprehend how many tears flowed from my eyes and never seemed to dry up. If only we could turn tears into renewable energy!

Whether you are grieving the loss of health, the loss of normality due to a disaster, the loss of a loved one, a relationship, or even a career, grief can consume the entire body and make it difficult to see a path toward ever feeling whole again.

My career has allowed me to share tender moments with those suffering from grief, sorrow, and loss—whether as a counselor present with a family before and after their loved one passes in hospice or as a social worker in the emergency room delivering difficult news to loved ones after a traumatic accident. I have also sat with clients making their way through a painful divorce, and listened to first-hand testimonials at international conferences of atrocities individuals and their families have endured during war. Grief is tangible and painful to observe, and while I cannot erase the pain and anguish for my clients, I know that the grieving process is essential to healthier healing. The body needs to express and process the deep pangs of loss. Feeling grief is not a sign of weakness, a surrender to fear, or a lack of faith. It is a natural healing balm for the body.

Some losses bring the type of grief that may last a lifetime. Grief can come as a result of things that we could never plan for or even comprehend. While healing is possible, grief can resurface at unexpected moments. Even though now, my life is wonderful and fulfilling, there are times, that grief will stop me in my tracks and I have accepted that grief will continue to resurface.

What Exactly is Grief?

Grief is a physical, emotional, and biological process that enlists all of our senses, allowing us to feel and respond to loss. It changes shape over time and may manifest as sadness, anger, guilt, shock, denial, depression, or any number of emotions.[1] Different stages of grief can arrive unexpectedly; there is no set order. Throughout this book, I have referred to anxiety and trauma as thieves that steal happiness and dreams. Grief, however, can benefit us as a benevolent teacher and a humble helper. As we grieve our losses, we learn how to increase our capacity to love and endure difficult things. Even in death, trauma, or loss, our love for others grows. Grief gives meaning as it mentors us on the fragility of life and the depth of our love and uses sorrow to bind us closer to others. We mourn and grieve best as communities, families, friends, and congregations.[2]

Grief is like an evergreen tree—the branches don't always grow evenly—and it is not the same for everyone. It can feel lopsided, heavy, and not equally divided. You may have more anger and less tears, while someone else has more tears and depression. It's not unusual to feel as if you've worked through grief and then be surprised when some random circumstance sets off an unexpected grief response. Human emotions and experiences can often be unpredictable, unfolding differently for everyone. In some of the happiest moments or times of celebration, you can feel a great sense of grief and loss, but at the same time feel grateful, happy, and joyful. Grief doesn't have to make sense. It doesn't have to start or end at certain places or times. It is similar to standing close to an evergreen tree. Far away, it looks uniform, shapely, and stately, but up close, branches of grief appear out of order, sappy, and frankly, not very pretty. Only when you step back do those misshapen branches take form, and the tree or grief is beautiful. When I stepped back, I could see my grief as more than stages of tears, depression, loneliness, anger, or other emotions, but rather as a whole process.[3] Stepping back, I could see that my grief was a reflection of the shape of my heart. The shape of your grief will reflect the love and goodness of your heart.

Grief and Denial

When I've experienced grief from a new loss, there have been times I felt stuck in a dream. Could I go to sleep, then wake up in the morning and my sorrow wouldn't exist? Denial is that sense that grief doesn't feel real or feels like a dream. It is a normal part of the grieving process, and denial can be a body's way of protecting you from a sharp loss. As time goes on, grief changes shape, and that denial can shift into any number of emotions. Grief helped me find new purpose, new goals, and new ways of living that I never expected. In a positive way, grief taught me to treasure relationships more deeply, increased my gratitude for wonderful moments in my life, and enlarged the awe I feel for the human spirit's ability to survive and be resilient, along with amplifying the empathy I feel for those who are suffering with heavy hearts.

Messengers of Grief

In a quote often attributed to Washington Irving, "There is a sacredness in tears. They are not the mark of weakness, but of power. They speak more eloquently than ten thousand tongues. They are the messengers of overwhelming grief, of deep contrition, and of unspeakable love."[4]

Tears are a beautiful gift our body gives us when grieving. Scientists have identified three different categories of tears: reflex, basal, and emotional tears. Depending on the physical purpose behind the tears, whether they are from anger, laughter, grief, or even slicing an onion, tears will consist of different chemicals. Reflex and basal tears physically protect our eyes from dust and debris; they are composed of 98% water.[5] Emotional tears can come from positive or negative emotions. These types of tears aid in hormone release, regulate stress levels, and reduce cortisol levels, helping the body return to a more balanced state.[6] In fact, researchers have established that crying releases oxytocin and endogenous opioids, also known as endorphins. These feel-good chemicals ease both physical and emotional pain and contain natural pain killers.[7] Please be patient and allow your body to grieve for as long as necessary, in whatever way suits you. Those unstoppable tears are trying to help you!

Grief and Depression

Losing my father was one of the deepest sorrows I have ever felt. In moments of grief, our memories become both a comfort and a longing. Grieving expert Deanna Edwards captured this sentiment in, *Grieving: The Pain and the Promise,* sharing "Photographs of dear ones passed help us face the transition from life to death."[8]

For me, that transition is softened by two images. One of my earliest photos captures me and my dad walking out of a donut shop in Boston soon after he became my father. In the photo, you can see the joy in my smile and skip in my step as we were beginning a new relationship and new adventure. And the last photo I have captures shortly before he passed. In his final week on Earth, despite the immense pain of cancer, my dad made a tremendous effort to attend my 40th birthday party. He rallied, joining our family as we stepped back in time--dressing in poodle skirts and jeans, dining at a 1950's diner, and bowling together. It was a profound act of selfless love of my dad, the sea captain, before crossing the bar.[9] Despite his pain, he chose to celebrate with me. His final gift—his presence—symbolized his entire life. His presence will be forever a treasure in my life.

One of the strangest things about grieving an expected loss was even though I had prepared for my father to pass, those preparations did not lessen the pain or shock of him actually being gone. The sadness and pain consumed me, and I fell into a grief-stricken depression. Losing the giant of a man who never made me feel small was a terrible shock. After his death, grief helped me reassess my thoughts, seeing even more of his love for me and our family. When he passed, the pain was more than I could have anticipated.

Death, divorce, retirement, illness, or other changes in our lives can bring sorrow-filled depression. We must make sense of our new world shaped by our losses. This depression can be part of the healing process. Don't hesitate to ask for help, join a support group, or find some books to read on grieving as you work through the process. You may find yourself talking to friends who are good listeners as you process the changes and sorrow. It has taken time for me to adjust to a new life without my father. The older I grow, the more my love continues to grow for him. I feel grateful to have him as a father. Russell M. Nelson said, "The only way to take sorrow out of death is to take love out of life."[10] Sorrow and grief would not exist without love. Grief and loss can cause seemingly incongruent experiences and feelings. The largest losses—the death of a child, the loss of a spouse, the end of a family through divorce—are all signs of love. Now whenever I look at the photos of my father, my heart still aches, but at the same time, it is full of joy for having such a wonderful father.

Grief and Injustice

Speaking of incongruent experiences, grief can also cause anger. When something feels unfair or violates our principles, anger is a natural reaction. Nevertheless, some may feel surprised that anger is part of grief and may feel it came out of nowhere. Trauma, grief, death, and loss seldom if ever feel fair. Anger is a completely normal reaction to loss.[11]

In any type of loss, it is good to acknowledge feelings of anger. Any type of grieving can trigger feelings of injustice, which then triggers anger, including:

- Feeling angry because of the timing of someone's death
- Feeling angry because someone else is suffering
- Feeling angry that you were robbed of a normal life due to an amputation or a life-changing illness
- Feeling angry at God for a miscarriage or death of a child
- Feeling angry about the situation survivors were left in after a disaster or war
- Feeling angry because of the way someone died
- Feeling angry at yourself for something you said or thought about the deceased
- Feeling anger towards family or friends for the way they responded to your loss
- Feeling punished for something you did not deserve
- Feeling forced out of a position

As we grieve, our minds can be focused on perceived injustices. A wife may say, "I am so mad at him for leaving me," even though logically she understands that her late husband didn't choose to have cancer or a heart attack. But the anger is real and needs to be processed, even if it seems illogical. One widow was surprised by her angry emotions after her husband death. He'd been very ill for months. When he passed away, it was a relief that he was no longer suffering. After his death, she found herself growing angry whenever she saw his large, size thirteen shoes. For some reason, seeing his shoes reminded her that they had not been able to retire together. She felt robbed. It wasn't fair he passed before they retired. One day, her anger drove her to pack up all his shoes and boots. She put them in the trunk of her car and dropped them off at a homeless shelter. As she gave away his shoes, the shape of her grief changed from anger to joy. Giving her husband's shoes to the homeless shelter was the last small offering she could give on behalf of her husband to a man who might desperately need size thirteen shoes. This removed some of the feeling of loss that he died before they could retire together. Grief offers unexpected healing.[12]

There are two parts of the brain that can respond when we feel angry—the impulsive, protective, chemical-releasing amygdala or the neural self-regulation, solution-centered system called the prefrontal cortex. The amygdala floods our body with hormones like cortisol.[13] One of the healthiest ways to handle anger and cancel out the hormone flooding is by acknowledging our anger aloud. Saying something as simple as, "I am feeling angry," helps halt the flood of hormones, and moves the process to the solution center. A friend of mine acknowledges her anger when she hits her head or stubs her toe by saying, "It's a good thing I don't swear." The simple act of acknowledging anger helps shift it from the emotional part of the brain, the amygdala, to the logical, executive function part of the brain, allowing us to act in a more rational, thoughtful manner.[14] This will help anyone feeling angry from grief or perceived injustices. Part of grieving is accepting anger as a valid emotion. Be okay with being angry and let it out in appropriate ways.

Don't Steal Another's Grief

Whether you are suffering a loss or supporting someone suffering a loss, an important key aspect of grief and recovery from loss is allowing whoever is carrying the grief to experience the entirety of the grieving process. Removing or attempting to shield someone from grief has the opposite effect. Rather than protect or shield them, intervening can rob them of the much-needed process that allows them to shed tears, create memories, and obtain closure. We don't always have control over what happens to us, but when we can control how we will face our losses, it allows us to move forward.[15] In my practice, I have witnessed clients who face the fire, so to speak, tackling what seems impossible and making what might be the hardest decisions of their lives—funeral arrangements, closing a business, letting go of possessions, or creating new living arrangements. We may be tempted to allow someone else to make decisions for us or us to make decisions for someone else going through a severe loss. It is interesting to note though that scientifically, such decisions use the executive function portion of the brain and aid in recovery of the one grieving. In a practical manner, creating solutions helps us grieve and find closure. Working through decisions and solutions helps grieving individuals process and structure new thoughts and emotions. In turn, this fosters growth in strength, ability, perspective, and appreciation. It is vital that we never take that away from someone, nor should we allow someone else to inadvertently take that from us.

Grief and Acceptance

Grief is its own dichotomy. In processing grief, I have found that happy experiences can be conflicting as they can be speckled with mourning. Moving forward and accepting the sorrow, changes, and loss can bring what I like to refer to as "weird spaces." One friend, whom I will call Sadie, shared the following story:

> *Annie and Mike were the dearest friends of Sadie and her husband. They celebrated holidays and spent almost every weekend together. They were such close friends that their babies napped in the same cribs if they were at one another's homes. One summer day, Mike passed away, shocking everyone and leaving Annie a young widow with three children.*
>
> *Eight years later, Annie met and married a wonderful man named Sam. On a perfect fall day, the wedding was a day of celebration and rejoicing. Annie was no longer alone. As she and Sam drove away, tin cans clanking along the ground, streamers hanging off their automobile, and the wedding party cheering, Sadie made eye contact with another close friend and tears filled their eyes at the same time. Without speaking, they understood. Mike was gone.*
>
> *Annie's daughter, now a young adult, saw this exchange and asked, "Why are you crying?"*

Sadie quickly brought a smile to her face and answered, "We are just so happy for your mom." It was true. They were happy for Annie's new life, but they also accepted the loss of Mike a little deeper that day.[16]

Grief has no set schedule. It can come at any time, in any order. It does not need to make sense, but no matter how it arrives, grief is a gift in the healing process.

Activities

1. Recall and write about a cherished memory with a loved one who has passed.
2. Look through old photos of someone who brought happiness and joy into your life. Reflect on the emotions you feel.
3. Write a heartfelt letter to a loved one you've lost, sharing updates on your life as if they were still here.

Sources

1 Ignacio, B. (2015, July 30). *The Seven Stages of Grief.* Social Work Tech. https://socialworktech.com/2012/11/13/the-seven-stages-of-grief/

2 Edwards, D. (1997). *Grieving: The Pain and the Promise.* p.18

3 Ignacio, B. (2015, July 30). *The Seven Stages of Grief.*

4 Dr. Boli, (2015, August 11). *Find the source of the quotation — Dr. Boli's celebrated magazine.* https://drboli.com/2015/08/11/find-the-source-of-the-quotation/ Note: This quote is attributed to Washington Irving and Dr. Johnson–neither can be authenticated.

5 Benisek, A. (2024, November 23). *Why We cry: The truth about tearing up.* WebMD. https://www.webmd.com/balance/why-we-cry-tearing-up

6 Gracanin, A., Bylsma, L. M., & Vingerhoets, A. J. J. M. (2014). Is crying a self-soothing behavior? *Frontiers in Psychology, 5.* https://doi.org/10.3389/fpsyg.2014.00502

7 Licsw, L. N. (2021, March 1). *Is crying good for you?* Harvard Health. https://www.health.harvard.edu/blog/is-crying-good-for-you-2021030122020

8 Edwards, D. (1997). *Grieving: The Pain and the Promise.* p.1

9 Lord Tennyson, A. (2024, June 22). *Crossing the bar.* The Poetry Foundation. https://www.poetryfoundation.org/poems/45321/crossing-the-bar

10 Nelson, R. M. (1992, April 2). *Doors of death.* https://www.churchofjesuschrist.org/study/general-conference/1992/04/doors-of-death?lang=eng#p7

11 Navarro, R., personal interview, August 2002.

12 Kearl, T., personal communication, 2008.

13 Goleman, D. (2018, March 8). *Remedy for rage: Tame your angry brain.* https://www.linkedin.com/pulse/remedy-rage-understand-your-angry-brain-daniel-goleman/

14 Goleman, D. 2019. Daniel Goleman: How to Short Circuit Anger | TJHS Ep. 232 (CLIP). https://www.youtube.com/watch?v=5na5mqpn7Rc

15 Edwards, D. (1997). *Grieving: The Pain and the Promise.* p.21

16 Anonymous, (2024). Friend of Author, T. Kearl.

CHAPTER 14

LOSS OF CONFIDENCE

Who Am I?

One of the hardest things was learning I was worth recovery.

— Demi Lovato

Before my traumatic experience, my life was happy. I was surrounded by supportive family, friends, and colleagues and had the career I had dreamed of. Between being a guest speaker at conferences, traveling, engaging in non-profit humanitarian work, and working with clients, this was the life I loved and fully expected to continue living.

It is odd—when you help others professionally, you never expect, or at least I never expected, to be on the other side needing help. Even with all the empathy, experience, and compassion from years of helping clients, I underestimated how deeply trauma could erode the confidence and core beliefs of someone from the inside. My loss of confidence was immediate and deep, unraveling all of the intentional effort I had invested over the years to build healthy self-confidence. I subscribed to Ryan Leak's insight: "Somewhere between insecurity and self-arrogance, we are looking for confidence."[1] My confidence was built on the belief that the work, education, sacrifice, and other efforts I had put into my life would protect me from life's storms. In the moment of trauma impact, my inner dialogue about my purpose, my strengths, and my expectations for myself and the future came crashing down. I felt worthless and vulnerable. The lack of self confidence from the trauma touched every part of my life, personally and professionally. The confidence I had worked so hard to build over the years through competence, self-improvement, personal growth, and spiritual learning was broken.

Trauma can break you, changing your relationship with yourself, your loved ones, your career, your hopes, and your dreams. Trauma undermined my identity. As a trauma therapist, I had walked with clients through their journey and witnessed them rise from the ashes of their lives into a phoenix—stronger, more vibrant, and more confident. Yet, in my own brokenness, I could not see hope for my future.

What is intriguing about a trauma response is it filters into areas of our life that perhaps aren't even associated with the traumatic event. As is with my personal experience. An example for me was public speaking. I had become comfortable with public speaking, but after my trauma, I felt fearful, panicked, and unqualified. How could trauma affect my self-confidence so deeply? After all the years of speaking in front of large audiences and helping others face their fears, I found myself doubting if I had anything valuable to say. How could something unrelated to speaking take away that aspect of my life? Trauma is a masterful thief!

The fight for my confidence and self-worth felt like walking against hurricane-force winds. In my mind, I could see and feel a great black wall that was trying to forcibly push me back and consume me. The black wall was telling me that I wasn't good enough, strong enough, safe, or worthwhile. My natural self at this point wanted to just dissolve and succumb to the darkness and negative messaging. But my deepest internal compass of self knew these messages were false and I couldn't give up. Deep down, I knew my happiness and future were worth fighting for.

Trauma can change thought processes and can form deep, immediate negative beliefs. These new pessimistic thoughts drive our emotions and affect our relationships and perception. Altered thoughts trauma victims experience can include:

- I don't know who I am
- I am unlovable
- I am not wanted

- I have no value
- I will never be good enough
- I can't protect myself
- I am stupid
- I am weak
- I don't know anything
- I am disposable
- I do not matter to anyone
- I can't stay safe
- I am not capable

One of the dangers of having low self-esteem or broken confidence is making it personal. Attending to and believing the distorted trauma-induced beliefs can lead to vulnerabilities, which in turn can extend trauma-based depression. Fighting the emotions of shattered confidence and self-esteem requires viewing yourself objectively from the outside. In a way, it is about removing your personal perspective, objectively sorting the lies from the trauma. As the negative thoughts arise, rebuilding comes by identifying our inner dialogue and what we are saying to ourselves. We can counter our negative thoughts and work at rebuilding our broken confidence by identifying true statements and changing the dialogue in our minds. Considering the truth of the inner dialogue will help us by countering the pervasive, permanent, and personal negative beliefs.[2]

It is heartbreaking to witness talented, loving, and capable individuals struggling to see their worth because trauma has eroded their soul and impacted their sense of self. While I now know more about the depths of the pain a client experiences due to the heavy burdens of distorted thinking and trauma-induced false beliefs, I also know there is healing ahead. There was a time when I lost my sense of self, not knowing who I was anymore. I could not envision regaining my old confidence or feelings of self-worth. The trauma stole my identity and confidence. The new challenge I faced was learning how to rebuild them. Thankfully, I did and so can you!

Activities

1. Ask a trusted friend to tell you of your strengths, gifts and talents.
2. Create a list of past talents and accomplishments. Write down how you can rebuild them.
3. Draw a picture of who you were before the trauma, how you look now, and a picture of your future confident self.

Sources

1 Leak, R. (2022). *Leveling up: 12 Questions to Elevate Your Personal and Professional Development.* Thomas Nelson. p.137.

2 Seligman, M. E. P. (1991). *Learned optimism.* Knopf. p.77.

CHAPTER 15

AVOIDANCE

The Running Man

Effective therapies require enhanced awareness of a sense of responsibility.

— Martin Seligman

Music and dancing are part of my happy place and an integral part of my personality. Dancing brings me joy. A popular dance move is known as the "running man." Thanks to the artistry of Janet Jackson and other hip-hop artists who popularized the fun street dance in western culture, it continues to remain a staple dance move in memes and social media.[1] The running man creates the perception the dancer is moving forward or going somewhere, but in truth there's no actual forward motion.

According to L. Kevin Chapman, shifting our attention away, or focusing on other things to avoid our emotions altogether, is not true problem solving.[2] When we avoid our emotions, we are essentially performing the running man dance. Avoiding emotions or emotional numbing, such as remaining emotionally distant or isolating ourselves from social interactions, can delay our progress and emotional healing. Suppressing emotions can cause them to come back with vengeance. Facing our emotions instead of avoiding them helps us protect ourselves.[3]

In the aftermath of trauma, certain isolating or protective behaviors may initially feel as if they are helping, but these coping mechanisms can be misleading. A week or two of these behaviors might not be a problem, but if such emotional avoidance goes on much longer, we need to be self-aware enough to recognize it so we can avoid its negative consequences.[4]

Some behaviors in our lives may be just like the running man–giving the illusion of moving forward or making progress while we're actually staying in the same place, avoiding emotions, difficult experiences, or fears. The examples in this chapter are only meant to offer insight and reflect a bare minimum of countless strategies we create to avoid emotions. Some standard avoidance actions can include:

- Burying emotions rather than discussing them
- Avoiding normal social activities or gatherings
- Remaining in bed or sleeping more than necessary
- Doom scrolling on phones or gaming
- Abusing alcohol, prescription medication, or other addictive substances
- Shopping or gambling addictions
- Focusing energy towards on online activities
- Cleaning or avoiding cleaning (it can be either)
- Shopping or avoiding shopping (again, it can be either)
- Deflecting with anger

After my initial traumatic experience, I was determined not to fall into a running man routine. One way to step out of avoidance is making plans. I planned and took a trip rather than staying stuck in the same place. It is vital that we take the time to identify any actions, habits, or behaviors that may prevent or block us from focusing on solving problems. My trip to Ireland was something I'd always wanted to do, as will be discussed in Chapter 16. While the trip itself was difficult in some respects and was not as well planned as I would have liked, it was not a wasteful experience. Changing my environment helped me gain some much-needed insight, courage, and confidence that I could do challenging things. You can too!

Whatever you choose to do does not necessarily need to be a big event! For some, spending a night home alone requires courage. Avoid the Running Man by doing something out of your comfort zone. It could be as simple as going for a walk instead of staying in the house. Visit an old friend. Speak to someone you don't generally interact with. Whatever you choose to do, move forward. Move your thoughts, your mind, and your body. Do anything out of your routine that improves your quality of life and fills your mind with new horizons. Stepping out of our comfort zone and breaking our normal patterns is one of the healthiest things we can do for our minds and our bodies. Incorporating new patterns into our routines is a way to stimulate new ideas, thoughts, solutions, and creativity.[5]

The running man illusion consists of habits that can sneak in at any time and covertly replace our normal life activities, thus stopping our progression, stunting our growth, and possibly costing us opportunities.[6] Such habits can interfere with relationships, substituting happiness and fulfillment with addictions or activities that help us avoid making real progress. Exceptional researcher George Valliant, PhD, identifies these types of behaviors as defense mechanisms.[7] Avoiding life does not make life easier or better. Facing life is a forward step out of the comfort zone.

When we become aware that we are falling into avoidance running man types of behavior, it's time to replace these steps with more constructive ones through intentional action. Visualizing the changes we want to see in our lives will help us to make the changes. After trauma, it requires a proactive approach to stay clear of avoidance behaviors. Recognizing the risks of isolation and other running man patterns during the *Clearing Phase* I intentionally created a schedule that included exercise and honored my commitments. If you notice yourself slipping, replace the comfortable steps of avoidance with bold and intentional actions.

Envision Transition: Grapevine

The grapevine is a basic dance sidestep that helps transition into new steps.[8] If we see ourselves not moving or progressing, we can work to envision ourselves stepping smoothly into new routines. Just like dancing, learning new steps requires courage. Instead of burying emotions, talk to someone about them. Scientists have learned that even if it's just a text message with a friend, these conversations are beneficial. In a social support study on perception, it was clear that those who had friends nearby or someone to speak with when facing an obstacle had a reduced perception of the level of difficulty of a task. While it did not change the actual difficulty of the activity, it *felt* less difficult.[9] If we are alone, obstacles, barriers and obstructions can appear more challenging than they actually are.

Martin Seligman submits that "Effective therapies require enhanced awareness of a sense of responsibility."[10] Making intentional choices to confront and face emotions enables us to develop a greater sense of control after a trauma *Storm.*

Intentional Steps

Instead of avoiding activities and staying home, take a small step and go somewhere. Even if it's just to a little shop or gas station, go somewhere and get yourself out of your routine. If you want to bury your emotions, take the bold step of texting someone you trust, or an even braver step of speaking to a counselor in person. If you catch yourself trying to avoid others, go for a drive, or call some friends over for an evening. When you notice yourself wanting to stay in bed, get up anyway. Do something, even if it's cleaning the glass on your bathroom mirror or making your house shine. If you are scrolling on your phone, playing games or tending to find online activities with no real merit, put the phone down and read a chapter of a book, or go for a walk. If you have the urge and realize you are reaching or thinking about addictive substances, remove them from your home and replace those habits with exercise and meditation.

Changing our dance steps or actions is our responsibility and will ultimately change our lives. Grab a friend or a family member if something looks too difficult. If you find yourself avoiding living, I invite you to grapevine, one step at a time, into any action that will improve your day-to-day living.

Activities

1. Evaluate if you have avoidant behaviors, if so, what are they?
2. Identify a new activity you would like to replace an avoidant behavior with.
3. Connect with past friends, current friends, online support groups, or mental health therapist.

Sources

1 Robertson, R. *(2010, February 2). Throwback: The running man. Essence.com. https://web.archive.org/web/20140714195310/http://www.essence.com/2010/02/02/throwback-the-running-man/*

2 Chapman, L. K. (2025, January 30). *Understanding emotional avoidance and learning to tolerate uncomfortable feelings.* Anxiety and Depression Association of America, ADAA. https://adaa.org/learn-from-us/from-the-experts/blog-posts/consumer/understanding-emotional-avoidance

3 Tull, M., PhD. (2023, November 16). *Emotional avoidance in PTSD.* Verywell Mind. https://www.verywellmind.com/ptsd-and-emotional-avoidance-2797640

4 Phoenix Australia. (2020, July 23). *Understanding Trauma | Phoenix Australia* [Video]. YouTube. https://www.youtube.com/watch?v=v60Pi87sqhI

5 Sanders, O. *(2025, January 15). Break the Routine: How to Dishabituate and reclaim your spark. eNotAlone. https://www.enotalone.com/article/personal-growth/break-the-routine-how-to-dishabituate-and-reclaim-your-spark-r21463/*

6 NeuroLaunch.com. (2024, November 1). *Emotional avoidance: recognizing, understanding, and overcoming patterns.* https://neurolaunch.com/emotional-avoidant/

7 Vaillant, G. E. (1994). Ego mechanisms of defense and personality psychopathology. *Journal of Abnormal Psychology, 103*(1), 44–50. https://doi.org/10.1037/0021-843X.103.1.44

8 Admin-Sfconservatoryofdance. (2024, April 25). Grapevine - Definition & Detailed Explanation - Dance Techniques Glossary - SFCOfDance. *sfconservatoryofdance.org.* https://sfconservatoryofdance.org/dance-techniques-glossary/grapevine/

9 Schnall, S., Harber, K. D., Stefanucci, J. K., Proffitt, D. R., University of Plymouth, Department of Psychology, Rutgers University at Newark, Department of Psychology, The College of William and Mary, & Department of Psychology, University of Virginia. (2008). Social support and the perception of geographical slant. In *Journal of Experimental Social Psychology* (Vol. 44, pp. 1246–1255) [Journal-article]. http://nwkpsych.rutgers.edu/~kharber/publications/Schnall.et.al.2008.Social%20Support%20and%20the%20Perception%20of%20Geographical%20Slant.pdf

10 Seligman, M. (2011). *What You Can Change... and What You Can't.* Hachette UK. p.241.

What are your thoughts from this Phase?

What would you like to change or implement moving forward?

CLEARING PHASE

Assessing Damage

Applying Resources

Rebuilding

When going through the Clearing Phase, life might feel overwhelming and daunting at times as you are actively trying to hold back the trauma impact that might include fear, darkness, anxiety, depression, brokenness and hopelessness. While at the same time putting energy into rebuilding your life with joy, faith, hope, peace, light and empowerment.

This drawing represents exactly how I felt during the Clearing Phase!

CHAPTER 16

CALM SAFE PLACE

My Field of Daisies

Your mind is like water. When it is agitated, it becomes difficult to see. But if you allow it to settle, the answer becomes clear.

— Master Oogway, Kung Fu Panda

During the intense *Storm* and *Clearing Phases,* heightened anxiety and safety concerns can make it difficult to achieve physical calm. I realized my body was always tense—with my hands clenched, my jaw tightened, and my legs shaking. Through my training I knew I had to focus on reversing the constant tension. For me, I found that taking intentional deep breaths while focusing on releasing the tension brings a sense of calm, peace and tranquility.

Creating calm is a conscientious choice. It requires deliberate focus, energy, intentional effort, and patience during the *Clearing Phase* and into the *Sunshine Phase.* This healing process does not always feel natural. Focusing on calming the body is important to reduce the release of cortisol and adrenaline triggered by the Four Fs: fight, flight, freeze, or fawn. Before my trauma *Storm,* it was natural to feel calm and peaceful. After the trauma *Storm,* during the *Clearing Phase* it became a daily struggle—a minute-by-minute effort—to keep my body in a calm state.

Additionally, I felt the need to create a calm and safe environment by having more control over my physical living space and time. My personal strategies to maintain this sense of control included actions like locking doors behind me, ensuring access to my own transportation, and practicing situational awareness. These steps allowed me to feel more in charge of my surroundings. Limiting time spent in certain spaces and controlling my schedule or events also helped. All of these behaviors, though seemingly simple, were ways of regaining a sense of safety and stability.

Anyone who has experienced a trauma *Storm* may find they have new physical and emotional boundaries that may be referred to as trauma-informed behaviors. These trauma informed responses help heal from trauma, along with aiding in engaging in daily and necessary activities, despite the obstacles they face. Recent research on trauma responses has shown that trauma responses reflect an individual's unique style of coping, and there is no single coping style that is better than another. The process of coping is complicated and should suit the needs of each individual.[1]

In my own response, being kind and non-judgmental to myself became an intentional effort to help me remain calm. At times, I believed some distorted thoughts, thinking that the changes I was making were signs of weakness. The truth was that those adaptations and changes were ways to gently help myself feel calmer and safer. Allowing ourselves to make choices about our environment reduces anxiety and increases empowerment.[2] With time, the behaviors might shift, but for now, it is best to embrace the new reality.

Nature's Healing Power

Across all cultures and eras, humanity has recognized the healing power of nature.[3] The Greek physician and philosopher Hippocrates wisely noted that, "Nature itself is the best physician."[4] When recovering from trauma, incorporating nature into the healing process offers valuable benefits and enhances the overall experience.[5] During my healing process, the mountains near my home became a place of refuge. Winding through mountain passes, hiking into the woods, and sitting by a river were times of peace and solace. The trees, the fresh scent of mountain air, and the sounds of nature grounded me, bringing a healing calm to my anxious spirit.

After a trauma, it is good to find your own places of peace and solitude. Some may find it in working on a physical project. One man found his solitude in the frigid winter air splitting logs and stacking cords of wood. Yours may be at a windy beach or sitting under a single tree, a favorite park bench, or a peaceful fountain. Dr. Gregory Bratman and his colleagues from the University of Washington found that contact with nature is linked with greater happiness, improved well-being, increased positive emotions, and more social interactions. A connection with nature also provides a deeper sense of purpose while helping reduce mental stress. Spending time in nature can reduce stress, enhance concentration, and improve mood, along with numerous other benefits, all of which are helpful when recovering from trauma.[6]

Intentional Change of Scenery

Every part of the body, from cells to muscles to organs, carries the weight of memories. This interconnectedness often results in prolonged illnesses or complicated recoveries. When the mind shuts down emotionally, the body can shut down as a way to physically protect itself.[7] The body and mind are renewed and strengthened by change. One helpful tool for promoting healing is changing your usual surroundings to create a calming and restorative environment. When seeking a calm or safe environment after trauma, intentionally changing the scenery to a peaceful space can help the body reset and relax.

For some, a road trip to a favorite camping spot or a visit to a friend can offer the change of scenery needed for recovery. The change doesn't need to be a big or extraordinary trip. Even small shifts in your environment can be powerful. Not everyone has the opportunity to change their scenery, even temporarily, but I cannot stress enough the importance of finding a safe, calm place in recovering from trauma. The English proverb, "A change is as good as a rest," holds true for trauma recovery during the *Clearing Phase.*

Changing our scenery is a good way to calm the body and reset the nerves. *New York University* psychologist Catherine Hartley explains that adding something novel to our routines is beneficial not merely for the day you change your routine, but for days afterward. Our neural circuitry is changed by traveling to unfamiliar sights and having new experiences.[8]

Stuck In A Trauma Loop

During the middle of my trauma *Storm*, I experienced physical and emotional changes, with my weight dropping to the lowest it had ever been as an adult. The unrelenting anxiety, the panic attacks, and the constant sense of fear were wearing down my body and soul. I recognized I needed a change — to find a calm space away from my usual places to reset and gather my thoughts and assess the damage from the trauma. I wanted to move forward, but I was stuck in a repetitive trauma loop, reliving certain events. One way to break a trauma loop is to change familiar routines or patterns, disrupting the cycle, and creating space for healing. With my training and background in trauma, I knew if I did not do something to change this loop, it could become persistent and harder to overcome.[9] I felt an urgent physical and emotional need to go somewhere new and break out of my routine. Gathering my courage, I pursued a lifelong dream. I had always envisioned traveling to Ireland to see the Cliffs jutting into the ocean and the beautiful countryside. I imagined dancing in lively Irish pubs and embracing the whole experience. This long-standing bucket list goal was inspired by my New Hampshire upbringing, where I was fortunate to grow up among Irish friends who shared their culture and traditions. Ireland felt like the perfect place to breathe deeply, find calm, and connect with nature. With the thoughts of changing scenery, I booked a flight, took a week off work, and headed to Ireland by myself to quiet the thoughts and feelings swirling within me.

I will always be glad I did this, but it was not an easy time. I have been a frequent international traveler, but this was my first time traveling internationally by myself. The change of scenery at such a vulnerable time was a strange but wonderful experience. It took real effort to balance my need to feel empowered, and quiet all the trauma thoughts and fears, but I felt proud of myself for taking on the challenge and going after something that I instinctively knew would help me ground myself. For someone else, the challenge may be hiking to the top of a mountain, learning a new skill like cake decorating or wood carving, paragliding, exploring a new place, or going to a museum alone.

Whatever, you decide to do—choose something meaningful that speaks to you. It will require courage, patience, and fortitude, but you have it within you to accomplish it.

Keep in mind, whatever you choose may not turn out exactly how you envision it, my trip did not, thanks to lingering Covid-19 restrictions. There were no lively pubs. Nevertheless, the trip allowed me to work through some significant thoughts and emotions, allowing me time for reflection and a distraction free atmosphere provided the tranquility to sort out my thoughts. One unexpected bonus from my trip, I re-gained some confidence. Some of the doubts and fears instilled by the trauma *Storm* were pushed back. Ireland is once again on my bucket list. I look forward to returning when I am in a calmer state ready to experience all the lively dancing and vibrant Irish pubs and connect with the locals.

Not everyone can take off work; in fact, many people experiencing trauma may have limited resources. A young mother found an early morning lap swim to be her safe place where the silence of the water wrapped around her like a protective cocoon and offered a sense of serenity and calm. A 60-year-old man, traumatized by near suffocation during a COVID-19 brush with death, developed panic attacks. After a month-long hospitalization, he was a shell of his former self and could no longer work or do physical labor. Though frail, he could sit up and offered to fix a sewing machine for a friend. In doing so, he found his quiet, calm space in the corner of a room fixing sewing machines. That little corner of his home with its familiar tools became his sanctuary where he felt safe and grounded. Whether it's an early morning walk, crafting, or a trip to the beach, identifying a safe, quiet, solitary place is essential. It is a key step to restoring balance to your body and mind.

Envisioning a Calm, Safe Place

One beneficial mindfulness strategy I've used for myself and with clients is creating a mental image of a calm, safe place. Imagining a calm, safe place is widely used in Eye Movement Desensitization and Reprocessing (EMDR) therapy and other therapeutic settings. This type of practice helps foster relaxation and emotional regulation or grounding.

During my healing, I developed three different calm place scenarios or images I can draw upon when needed. The first is lying in a field in New Hampshire where I grew up, on a blanket surrounded by wild daisies with my horses, Honey and Cinnamon, grazing nearby. My body is comforted by the warmth of the sun, and I feel safe and at peace. Another calm place is floating effortlessly in Lake Sunapee, a favorite place of my formative years. My third peaceful image is floating weightlessly in a fluffy white cloud.

When I work with clients, I encourage them to share the different places they imagine. Some have a specific place in nature, while others imagine a single room, a place from their childhood, or a place they have visited. Some people imagine something creative, such as a rainbow or floating through space. As you form the images in your mind, it is important to create a space where you are the only person present, even if other people are normally there. *Below is a sample or practice version you can try.* If you would like additional resources, there are videos available online and phone apps that can guide you through a calm place mindfulness activity.

The **Calm Safe Place** exercise is a valuable tool used in therapy, designed to help individuals establish a mental sanctuary for relaxation and emotional regulation. This technique is particularly beneficial during trauma recovery, providing a mental refuge to manage distressing emotions.[10]

Suggested Steps to Create a Calm Safe Place:

1. **Find a Comfortable Space:** Sit in a comfortable position and take a few deep breaths to relax.
2. **Identify and Visualize a Safe Place:** Think of a place, real or imagined, where you feel completely safe, calm, and at peace. This could be a serene beach, quiet woods, or a cozy room. Sit in a comfortable position and take a few deep breaths to relax.
3. **Activate your Senses:**
   - **Sight:** Visualize the colors, shapes, and objects in this place.

- **Sound:** Imagine sounds you might hear, such as waves crashing or birds singing.
- **Smell:** Recall any fragrances associated with this place, like salty sea air or fresh mountain air.
- **Touch:** Feel the textures, such as soft sand underfoot or a gentle breeze on your skin.
- **Taste:** If applicable, imagine any tastes linked to this environment.

4. **Associate Positive, Happy Feelings:** Focus on the positive emotions that arise when you immerse yourself in this safe place. Allow feelings of calmness, safety, and relaxation to envelop you.
5. **Select a Cue Word or Phrase:** Select a word or short phrase that encapsulates the essence of your safe place (e.g., "peace," "serenity," or "calm retreat"). This cue can be used to quickly access the safe place in your mind when needed.
6. **Practice with Bilateral Stimulation (BLS) (Optional):** While focused on your calm, safe place, you may incorporate bilateral stimulation, such as tapping alternately on each knee or using guided eye movements.[11] This can enhance the connection to your safe place, though it's often guided by a trained EMDR therapist.
7. **Rehearse Accessing the Safe Place:** Regularly practice visualizing your safe place, especially during moments of calm, to strengthen your ability to access it during times of stress. Use your chosen cue word or phrase to facilitate quicker access. This word becomes a powerful anchor. It signals to your mind to return to the serene mental space you've created. It can also be reinforced by bilateral stimulation.

Whether you focus on deep breathing, spending time in nature, visualizing a calm and safe place, or other calming tools, these practices require dedication and trial and error as we hone our abilities. It does not usually come naturally or easily, especially after a traumatic experience.

As you experiment with different tools and resources, you will uncover transformative tools that have a lasting impact. Even though trauma changes us, we can grow stronger. We have the power to overcome trauma, emerge stronger, and live a healthy, happy life. All the work, effort, and concentration in these tools will help you to find peace and joy that will last a lifetime.

Activities

1. Find a calm, safe place for your body to relax, whether in the mountains, a scenic drive, a special place in your home, a swimming pool, etc.
2. Practice creating a calm, safe place in your mind using the technique in this chapter.
3. Think about a new place you would like to visit.

Sources

1 Center for Substance Abuse Treatment (US). Trauma-Informed Care in Behavioral Health Services. Rockville (MD): Substance Abuse and Mental Health Services Administration (US); 2014. (Treatment Improvement Protocol (TIP) Series, No. 57.) Chapter 3, Understanding the Impact of Trauma. Available from: https://www.ncbi.nlm.nih.gov/books/NBK207191/

2 Bobo, A. (2024, January 22). *Exploring Nature Therapy: a fresh start in the great outdoors for trauma survivors.* Wellview Counseling LLC. https://wellviewcounseling.com/exploring-nature-therapy-a-fresh-start-in-the-great-outdoors-for-trauma-survivors/

3 Weir, K. (2020, April 1). *Nurtured by nature: Vol. 51, No. 3 Print version: page 50.* https://www.apa.org. Retrieved January 13, 2025, from https://www.apa.org/monitor/2020/04/nurtured-nature

4 Smith, W. D. (2024, November 21). *Hippocrates | Biography, Works, & Facts.* Encyclopedia Britannica. https://www.britannica.com/biography/Hippocrates

5 Bynum, W. F. (2001). Nature's helping hand. *Nature, 414*(6859), 21.

6 Bratman, G. N., Anderson, C. B., Berman, M. G., Cochran, B., De Vries, S., Flanders, J., Folke, C., Frumkin, H., Gross, J. J., Hartig, T., Kahn, P. H., Kuo, M., Lawler, J. J., Levin, P. S., Lindahl, T., Meyer-Lindenberg, A., Mitchell, R., Ouyang, Z., Roe, J., . . . Daily, G. C. (2019). Nature and mental health: An ecosystem service perspective. *Science Advances, 5*(7). https://doi.org/10.1126/sciadv.aax0903

7 Woods, E. (2023, December 12). *A change of scenery to heal the body and the mind | CPTSDfoundation.org.* https://cptsdfoundation.org/2023/12/12/a-change-of-scenery-to-heal-the-body-and-the-mind/

8 Pattillo, A. (2024, February 20). *Scientists pin down a link between happiness and 1 daily activity.* Inverse. https://www.inverse.com/mind-body/new-experiences-shape-mood-study

9 Brain Retraining Program, re-origin®. (2023, July 17). *Breaking free from trauma loops (Neuroplasticity!)* [Video]. YouTube. https://www.youtube.com/watch?v=K4zjTwOs_Uw

10 McAdam, E. (2018, July 18). *Therapy in a Nutshell, Grounding exercise for anxiety #7: Creating a safe place* [Video]. YouTube. https://www.youtube.com/watch?v=Isw37iCwMCg

11 The Human Condition. (2022, January 21). *Bilateral stimulation: definition, methods, benefits, and effectiveness.* https://thehumancondition.com/bilateral-stimulation/

CHAPTER 17

COMFORT & WEIGHTED BLANKETS

Bring Me My Minky

A cozy blanket is like a warm embrace for the soul.

— Unknown

No matter how old someone may be, a cozy blanket can bring comfort and calm. We might picture children clinging to their "blankies" as they carry them around or a grandma with her favorite quilt on her lap. We may recall Linus from Charlie Brown cartoons protecting his well-loved security blanket or envision a child wrapped in their favorite quilt. Even as you read this, you may be thinking of a favorite childhood blanket or one you currently love. According to Cambridge Dictionary, a blankie is "a piece of material that makes [someone] feel safe and happy."[1] Over the years, I have found that blankets are the most commonly used comfort tools among my clients working through their *Trauma Impact Phases.*

The use of blankets dates back to 3000 BC.[2] More recently, weighted blankets have gained widespread attention for their ability to comfort trauma patients, support chemo patients during infusions, and improve sleep for children with ADHD.[3] The pressure from a weighted blanket can regulate your autonomic nervous system. It eases symptoms of anxiety, lowers heart rate, slows breathing, and creates a calming effect.[4] It also promotes the release of calming chemicals like serotonin, which counteracts the hormones cortisol and adrenaline.[5]

During my healing process, I relied on one of my favorite blankets to calm my anxious body down and feel a sense of peace. At times,

I completely covered my head and body like a cocoon to feel secure. During my recovery, I kept an extra blanket in my car to help manage my anxiety when I was away from home. On nights of intense anxiety, I would drive to the mountains, find a quiet place to park, wrap up in my blanket, and gaze at the stars. Feeling safe and secure, I sat in my car listening to music under a beautiful star covered-sky. Over the years, my blankets have absorbed many tears and played a significant part in my healing.

My favorite blankets come from Minky Couture (*www.softminkyblankets.com),* a company known for creating its ultra-soft, high-quality plush blankets. My friend, Sandi Hendry, founded the company during a family crisis when her adult daughter faced a life-threatening illness. Sandi wanted to create an adult blanket with the same cozy, soft features of a baby's favorite blanket. Friends and family loved them so much that demand quickly skyrocketed. Today, the company has sold millions of blankets.[6] This is a powerful example of the silver linings that can emerge from trauma—a simple desire to give a gift to her daughter has now brought comfort to millions. Silver linings that stem from trauma are all around us, if we look for them. No matter the type of trauma you are facing, do not underestimate the comfort and healing a favorite or a weighted blanket can provide. It can help your body feel supported, grounded, and calm throughout the healing journey.

Activities

1. Can you recall a special blanket you have had in your life? What are some of the memories associated with the blanket?
2. Purchase a new blanket in a color and style that helps you feel peace.
3. Place blankets in areas you might experience anxiety, such as your car, office or different rooms in your home.

Sources

1 *blankie.* (2025). https://dictionary.cambridge.org/us/dictionary/english/blankie

2 Sheezie. (2022, July 20). Who Invented Blankets? [When, Where & How]. *Nevada Inventors.* https://nevadainventors.org/who-invented-blankets/

3 Eron, K., Kohnert, L., Watters, A., Logan, C., Weisner-Rose, M., & Mehler, P. S. (2020). Weighted Blanket Use: A Systematic review. *American Journal of Occupational Therapy, 74*(2), 7402205010p1-7402205010p14. https://doi.org/10.5014/ajot.2020.037358

4 *Ackerley, R., Olausson, H., & Badre, G. (2015). Positive effects of a weighted blanket on insomnia. ResearchGate. https://www.researchgate.net/publication/279846113_Positive_effects_of_a_weighted_blanket_on_insomnia*

5 Cherry, K. (2024, June 17). *What is the Fight-or-Flight response?* Verywell Mind. https://www.verywellmind.com/what-is-the-fight-or-flight-response-2795194

6 Brewer, H. (2024, June 24). *Heart of Minky Story - The origin and legacy of Minky Couture.* Minky Couture. https://www.softminkyblankets.com/blogs/blog/heart-of-minky-story-the-origin-and-legacy-of-minky-couture

CHAPTER 18

COMMUNITY & MENTORS

Structuring Our Reinforcements

I have role models, but I take the attributes of the people that I admire, and I use them to create my best self.

— Marley Dias

Role Models/Mentors

No matter who we are or where we come from, we all look to role models to help shape our behavior and values and guide the direction of our growth. One of the most interesting discoveries of the 1990s was the existence of unique brain cells that can activate in one of two ways: when someone performs an action or when they observe someone else performing an action. These brain cells, known as *mirror neurons,* light up like a disco ball in the 1970s when activated.[1] Well, maybe not really a disco ball—but you get the idea.

Initially discovered in Macaque monkeys, researchers now suspect that most animals have some version of mirror neurons, as most living creatures appear to learn from observation.[2] What is so exciting about our disco ball neurons is the fact that when we see others do good things, it leaves an impression on our minds. Humans are hardwired to learn through our shared connections. According to social learning theory, we learn best by observing others who encourage us and reinforce our belief in ourselves.[3]

In 1999, Chartrand and Bargh discovered the chameleon effect, which explains how we subconsciously imitate or mimic the behaviors of leaders. Athletes subconsciously begin to imitate their coaches. Children imitate their parents. Students imitate their teachers.[4] This unintentional mimicry demonstrates the value of good role models. When we experience trauma, we can look to our role models for guidance. Seeing or remembering the strength with which others have met their challenges becomes our frame of reference for how we should meet our own.

There are countless people throughout history, in the news, and in our lives who can be personal examples of hope as we go through the healing process. While working through my own recovery, I would picture former clients who had gone through severe traumatic experiences. I witnessed their strength, resilience, and perseverance as they worked through painful events like the death of a child, the loss of a spouse, or the development of disabilities. I attended United Nations meetings where trafficking survivors shared their firsthand accounts of atrocities, and others shared reports of crimes and attacks that took place during horrific wars and genocides. I listened to victims of oppressive and abusive societies and deadly poverty, as well as people who needed to flee their homes, leaving everything behind. In working with these refugees who sacrificed so much and had to begin their lives over again, I witnessed a level of resiliency that defies logic. Watching and hearing the stories of so many people determined to heal and create a brighter story for themselves helped me know that I, too, could overcome trauma.

As I looked for my mentors and role models, I included some within my spiritual belief system. Women in the Bible such as Rebecca, Mary, and Hannah lived with courage and continue to serve as wonderful role models. Deborah's courage, wisdom and leadership particularly resonate with me. She served as a judge and faithful religious leader, and when faced with what seemed a lost cause, she reminded the military leader Barak to have faith in the promises of the Lord. Many of her qualities spoke to me deeply. This led me to look for artists' renderings of Deborah with her sword and shield, that I put on my phone, along with some quotes I could easily access.

When I was feeling helpless, broken, or discouraged, I would look at the picture of Deborah and read quotes about her, which gave me strength and a renewed desire to push forward. Deborah was not only a leader during wartime who brought forty years of peace to her people, she remained brave, wise and optimistic despite devastation surrounding her, including the possible destruction of her people. Facing iron chariots, she chose the counter-intuitive path and faced them head on.[5] She was a true valiant warrior.

Although I was not fighting a physical war, my body and mind felt like I was at war with my trauma and the devasting scars. The battle felt destructive, but I knew I wanted to be triumphant just as Deborah had been. One of the pictures and quotes I saved was of Deborah kneeling. It said, *"When God's warriors go down on their knees, the battle is not over. It has just begun."*[6]

I often found myself on my knees in prayer, pleading for strength, and at times all I could muster was a pleading, *"Please help me."* In those moments, I realized I had two choices: crumble into nothingness or rise and be triumphant. I chose to be triumphant! But I also knew it would take a great deal of strength and effort on my part, and I relied on the images and examples of Deborah to strengthen my faith and hope, even when things seemed terribly hopeless.

Across all belief systems we may feel drawn to a variety of role models who align with our individual needs and goals, but it's essential to seek out mentors. Thes may come from fictional figures, like Éowyn from Tolkien's *The Lord of the Rings* to current or historical individuals. We are constantly surrounded by inspiring role models who are examples of strength and encouragement.

Community

Along with role models, it is important to find a community of people who can support, listen, encourage, and guide us during our healing. For some, this is very natural as they already had a great support system in place before the trauma. One of my greatest blessings in my life is having amazing family and friends who were supportive and present with me during my traumatic experience and healing. My community contributed a great deal to my surviving and healing. They held me up at times when I couldn't hold myself up. The night of my traumatic experience, I walked into the home of loved ones and immediately crumbled to the floor. My loved ones scooped me up and comforted me, and that was my first step toward surviving.

In *The Happiness Advantage,* Shawn Achor shares, "Countless studies have found that social relationships are the best guarantee of heightened well-being and lowered stress, both an antidote for depression and a prescription for high performance."[7] Moreover he adds, "The most successful people turn inward; they actually hold tighter to their social support. Instead of divesting, they invest. Not only are these people happier, but they are more productive, engaged, energetic, and resilient. They know that their social relationships are the single greatest investment they can make in the Happiness Advantage."[8]

One day when I was looking for a show to watch on Netflix, I was drawn to a show called *Live to 100: Secrets of the Blue Zone.* The study focused on finding the reasons why specific areas—so-called "blue zones"—around the world were healthier than the average. During their series, they found that two factors contributing to healthier lives were family relations and social circles. In my practice, I have seen the difference it makes in the process of healing from trauma and thriving emotionally when these relationships are developed in healthy ways. If you're interested in learning more, the group who studied the blue zones also has a website: *www.bluezones.com.*[9]

Some individuals, though, may not have developed a healthy support system before trauma, and this can be challenging. When I work with clients with limited support, I encourage them to find safe online community groups, therapy support groups, religious or spiritual groups, or local community groups with a common interest. Intentional relationship building is critical, as the benefits are worth the investment of time and energy.

Loneliness

Trauma recovery can feel very lonely as you work through the *Trauma Impact Phases.* As time goes on, survivors—even those who have the strongest support systems—may begin to feel like a burden to others. We can feel like we need to put on a fake smile or withhold our thoughts to protect others from discomfort. We may want to be more positive, so we don't continue to feel like we are "bleeding" on others. Since the healing process can sometimes take years, those around us may feel anxious for us to be happy and heal faster. This comes from a good place, as we all desire for the people we love to be happy, thrive, and see how amazing they are. Unfortunately, like a broken body part, trauma healing has its own timeline. We do all we can to promote healing, but the mind and heart have a natural process they need to work through.

As a reassurance, when sitting with a therapy client, I have never thought, "I just wish they could get over the trauma and be happy and just heal quicker." However, I can't say I have always been that patient with my loved ones. My sister went through a heartbreaking divorce just a year before me. I remember feeling anxious for her after about nine months. I wanted her to find her way, feel happier, recognize her own worth, and regain her confidence. My intentions were good—I just wanted to see her happy again, thriving, and ready to take on the world. However, her body still had a lot of processing and healing to do.

Be patient with the process and with your social support. Trauma is a learning experience. Looking from the outside in, it is difficult to see the depth of damage that someone has experienced. Just because we want the body to heal quicker doesn't mean it will. Patience with yourself and others, as well as understanding the challenges of trauma and the time it takes to work through the *Clearing Phase,* can make you a compassionate mentor to those on their healing journey.

Personal and Relationship Growth

Don't lose hope in the healing process. As you apply intentional efforts and resources, trauma can transform into hope and healing. Personal growth and relationships can be strengthened. As Achor concluded in his book, "After trauma, people also report enhanced personal strength and self-confidence, as well as heightened appreciation for, and greater intimacy in, their social relationships."[10] During the *Clearing Phase,* look for mentors. Look for individuals you aspire to become. Seek out individuals whose qualities you admire and aspire to embody. With time, you will begin to mirror them and their strengths.

Activities

1. Create a list of strengths you admire in others.
2. Create a list of individuals you look to in life, literature, or history who have demonstrated those strengths.
3. Spend some time researching a favorite mentor: Find quotes, pictures, or artwork that represent their strengths.

Sources

1 Kilner JM, Lemon RN. (2013) What we know currently about mirror neurons. Curr Biol. 2013 Dec 2;23(23):R1057-62. doi: 10.1016/j.cub.2013.10.051. PMID: 24309286; PMCID: PMC3898692.

2 Miklósi, Á. (2024, February 20). Do dogs have mirror neurons? *Scientific American.* https://www.scientificamerican.com/article/do-dogs-have-mirror-neurons

3 Mathew, A. (2024, June 1). The Power of Role Modeling: How Leaders Impact Our Brains & Behaviors. *Peoplekult.* https://www.peoplekult.com/post/the-power-of-role-modeling-for-leaders

4 Chartrand, T. L., & Bargh, J. A. (1999). The chameleon effect: The perception–behavior link and social interaction. *Journal of Personality and Social Psychology, 76*(6), 893–910. https://doi.org/10.1037/0022-3514.76.6.893

5 King James Bible. (1979). Judges 4.

6 Fronk Olson, C. (2009). *Women of the Old Testament.* Deseret Book. p.

7 Achor, S. (2018). *The happiness advantage: How a Positive Brain Fuels Success in Work and Life.* Crown Currency. p.14.

8 Achor, S. (2018). *The happiness advantage: How a Positive Brain Fuels Success in Work and Life.* Crown Currency. p.175.

9 Buettner, D. (2023). *Watch Live to 100: Secrets of the Blue Zones | Netflix official site.* Retrieved February 5, 2025, from https://www.netflix.com/title/81214929

10 Achor, S. (2018). *The happiness advantage: How a Positive Brain Fuels Success in Work and Life.* Crown Currency. p.110.

CHAPTER 19

DANCING

My Own Dancing Queen

Dance like there's nobody watching.

— William Purkey

As you might have read in my bio, I love to dance! My friends and family refer to me as the "dancing queen," since I not only love to dance, but also love ABBA's music. I even have a T-shirt that says, "*Dancing Queen*!" Being born in the 1970s, I have happy childhood memories of dancing to disco music, but I'll dance to anything with a beat. When I was about seven years old, my mom worked at Arthur Murray Dance Studio in Jacksonville, Florida. This meant I could go over and dance to the music in front of the large mirrors. It felt like a young girl's dream come true. In my young mind, I was a professional, beautiful dancer!

Dancing has always been a positive coping skill for me, and I can feel my body shift into a more positive space when I dance. This is because dancing, like many forms of exercise, releases endorphins. Endorphins are naturally occurring chemicals in the brain. They work to diminish pain and increase pleasure, thus helping reduce symptoms of depression and anxiety and improve self-esteem.[1]

Now, don't get the idea that I am a great dancer, because I am not! I have never been formally trained, and I may not be the most graceful, but I have fun, and I love dancing. It makes me happy and uplifts my soul and spirit!

While in the *Storm Phase*, I felt like my body was going to burst from the anxiety and stress stored in my cells. I knew I needed to release that energy, so I was very intentional about dancing, whether in the car, at home, or at a concert. At the time, it was difficult to feel happiness like I usually did, and dancing helped take the edge off before I imploded from stress and sadness. I would come home from work and put on my favorite songs and dance like nobody was watching—and nobody was! I would dance on the counters, on the couch, and on the table. I would purposely take up as much space in the room as possible with my footwork, twirls, and leaps. Perhaps I needed a movie moment like Tom Cruise in *Risky Business*! By doing this, I felt more in control of my body and how I wanted to express my emotions while releasing boiling energy.

During my recovery, I intentionally attended concerts or dance venues to feel free and dance unabashedly. It was liberating to let my body release the sadness and trauma, embracing feelings of happiness and getting lost in the moment. In the beginning of my healing process, I booked a flight out of state to see a Jungle live concert with my adult kids. I had never heard Jungle's music before, but my kids thought I would love their music, and they were right! It was evident that I was one of the oldest attendees, but I danced the night away with the young crowd. The band had a disco vibe, which I loved, of course! Jungle plays to the energy of the crowd creating a connection that makes you want to keep moving. After the concert ended, there was a small group that continued dancing for every possible second until they were invited to leave. That was my group. It was fun to be called the "cool" mom and share this night with my kids. That was super flattering and of course, filled me with joy, *but what no one knew was I was dancing for my life*. I was fighting to create light and happiness. It truly felt like a physical battle. Leaving the trauma *Storm* behind, I was determined to rewrite my own story—refusing to let the darkness define me.

Soon after the Jungle concert, I attended an Odesza concert with my kids, and we all dressed up in sparkly, shimmering clothes. I even adorned my face and hair with sparkles. Why not? That night, my girls even taught me how to dance with a light rope, which is super fun.

I danced and sang at the top of my lungs with songs I loved. I wanted to feel free and lose the chains that felt so heavy on my body. The healing benefits of dancing continue to serve me as I attend dance nights at local venues. My body needs it, so I am intentionally putting it into my story. Dancing makes me feel more alive, happy, and myself. I feel myself continuing to heal when I dance.

Dancing has been a part of the world for thousands of years and is embedded into our cultures and society. No matter their age, ability or where they live, the beat of a song seems to move people. Dance is a natural, built-in therapeutic tool for healing and positive social interactions. It can improve certain aspects of memory, emotional well-being, depression, and even social cognition.[2] I have often wondered if part of why anxiety and depression have increased is that we have taken dance out of our modern culture as adults. Before modern times, community dance halls, barn-raising dances, church dances, and more were key gathering places and events in our communities.

Dancing might not be for everyone! But what I want you to think about is what makes you feel alive. What gives you this type of happiness? I encourage you to add that into your healing process!

Some of Kelli's Favorite Dance Songs

"On the Floor" by Jennifer Lopez and Pitbull
"Levitating" by Dua Lipa and DaBaby
A variety of Pink songs
Of course – ABBA songs

Activities

1. Create a dance playlist that makes you feel happy.
2. Attend a dance or concert.
3. Sign up for some type of dance lessons.

Sources

1 University of Sydney. (2024, February 12). *Dancing may be better than other exercise for improving mental health.* University of Sydney News. https://www.sydney.edu.au/news-opinion/news/2024/02/12/dancing-may-be-better-than-other-exercise-for-improving-mental-h.html

2 University of Sydney. (2024, February 12). *Dancing may be better than other exercise for improving mental health.* The University of Sydney. https://www.sydney.edu.au/news-opinion/news/2024/02/12/dancing-may-be-better-than-other-exercise-for-improving-mental-h.html

CHAPTER 20

GOALS & VISION

Developing the Life I Want

Without goals and plans to reach them,
you are like a ship that has set sail with no destination.

— Fitzhugh Dodson

My journey in healing has been about intentionally taking back the pen and writing my own story, understanding that my destination and happiness are in my own hands. After my trauma *Storm,* how does one begin to start rebuilding? Just like building a house, I needed to start with architectural drawings that would guide my steps in building the new structure.

Thankfully, being goal-oriented and a planner comes naturally to me. I know that is not the case for everyone. Through the years, I have been labeled "a mover and a shaker" because I love setting goals and meeting them. But never had I faced the overwhelming task of rebuilding such a significant structure, especially while struggling emotionally. I wasn't just building a single room. I was building a whole house and needed the vision, goals, and plans in order to begin. It felt daunting but absolutely necessary. Trauma can blur our belief that we have the strength and ability to accomplish our hopes and dreams. This is especially true when our life's circumstances have drastically changed due to lifestyle, physical limitations, death of a loved one, or other things out of our control. Combined with the physical and emotional exhaustion that comes with trauma, considering or setting new goals can seem impossible.

For continued healing, we need to dig deep and apply self-determination as we fight for our new normal and prove to ourselves that we have choices and control of our path. This was absolute truth for me as I sought the emotional strength to rebuild the destroyed parts of myself and continue to grow in all aspects of my life.

One activity my clients enjoy is imagining themselves at ninety years old, sharing their life story. They reflect on all they have accomplished in their lifetime. The directive is that they have all the money they want, no limitations, and no fears or anxiety. The client then identifies their deepest desires for their life, and what really matters to them. Most of the time, when people work on goals, they identify something they would like, but then quickly shut it down due to perceived limitations. For example, someone may say they want to travel, but then quickly follows it up with barriers, such as not having enough money, needing to work, feeling like they wouldn't have anyone to go with, or even simply stating, "Good things like that don't happen for me."

When setting goals, I implore you not to shut down opportunities. Instead, put belief in your capabilities to influence outcomes. One of my greatest thrills as a therapist has been seeing clients meet unexpected goals: starting and completing college when they didn't feel they had the capabilities, finding strength and resources to leave an abusive relationship, hiking a mountain when they didn't feel they had the physical ability, changing a career path, and adapting their finances to be happier, and many others. For me, my goal was to write a book when I didn't believe I had the skill set, knowledge, or patience to do it. My belief is that we are all more capable than we believe and that we have more control over our choices than we allow.

S.M.A.R.T goals are clear, measurable targets to aim for during the *Clearing* and *Sunshine Phases.* Research shows we succeed most frequently when our goals are S.M.A.R.T. goals, meaning they are specific, measurable, achievable, relevant, and time-bound.[1] Small or large, goals should be very specific. Whether you are breaking a large goal into smaller sections or setting smaller goals to begin with, this process helps us move forward from traumatic experiences and rewire our brains. Envisioning the changes we want to make and the goals we'd like to achieve, writing them down, and creating a plan of action are all part of the healing process.

During the *Clearing Phase,* I began to design plans for my new structure. I created a vision board on a big bulletin board that outlined my vision and goals. My goals were specific. The board was displayed in my study, allowing me to see it multiple times a day. In the morning, I would check in to remind myself of my vision and then check in again at night to see what I accomplished that day. On the board, I broke down my goals into specific categories that included family, friends, finances, physical, emotional, spiritual, fun, interests, and career. Then, under each category, I added specific goals that would help me build the life I wanted and become the person I wanted to be.

Along one side of the board, I added statements to remind myself of my value, such as: *I am worthy, I am valuable,* and *I am resilient.* On the other side of the board, I wrote words of encouragement, including: *Let go of fear, Enjoy the journey, I can do hard things,* and *Make your dreams come true.* In the middle of my vision board, I included quotes that spoke to my soul and inspired me and then, at the bottom of the board I added some of my guiding life values—*Hope, Joy, Faith,* and *Peace.* To make the board feel connected to my personality, I decorated the board with a butterfly, a compass, a peacock feather, jewels, flowers, and of course some glitter lettering. This vision board encapsulated what I wanted my life to look and feel like. It became the plans for my new structure.

With each goal, I came up with specific details to help me set S.M.A.R.T. goals in a way I could achieve. Below is an example of a S.M.A.R.T. goal for someone who wants to improve their physical fitness:

- **Specific:** "I am going to walk for 30 minutes every day before I go to work."
- **Measurable:** "My goal is to lose 24 pounds this year, which is 2 pounds per month or 8 ounces per week."
- **Achievable:** "I will stop hitting the snooze button and sit up before turning off the alarm."

- **Relevant:** "I want to live a longer and healthier life and have more energy and strength."
- **Time-bound:** "I will do this for the next four months until the weather changes. In September, I will buy a six-month membership to the recreation center."

For one of my goals, I wanted to be more connected to family and friends. I wrote out specific names and how many times a month I wanted to visit. To follow through, beyond my paper plans, I then acted. I contacted my friends and family and scheduled time with them on my calendar. Another goal was to take some lessons to learn new skills that would make me happy, so I chose figure skating lessons since it was something I had always wanted to do. I looked for a rink and an instructor and secured the lessons on my schedule, along with a line-item expense in my budget. I am not a great skater, but I love knowing a few fun moves on the ice and am proud of meeting a lifetime goal. These goals gave me confidence and helped me feel more alive, and like I was progressing in things I wanted to achieve.

There is excitement in working towards developing the life we want and becoming the person we want to be. That can look very different for each person since we are each on our own individual journey. The path begins with the vision, followed by taking intentional steps toward that goal, no matter how small. When I felt drawn to write this book, all I could see was how daunting the project would be, how many words I would need to write, the vulnerability in sharing my story, and the doubts of whether the content would even be helpful and how the book would be judged. But ultimately, I knew it was something I would regret not doing. I needed it to be part of the story I will tell when I am ninety years old. So, it began, one word at a time until a sentence was completed, a paragraph formed, sections unfolded, and a book was published.

You may have heard that it takes twenty-one days to create a new habit. However, researchers have discovered that it actually takes four continuous periods of twenty-one days to create, establish and secure a new habit. During those 84 days, your brain creates new neural connections while gradually releasing old behavior patterns. If counting days feels overwhelming, simply think in terms of three months, or 12 weeks. There are two especially challenging phases within the 84-day journey of creating new habits, goals and visions. The first often arises between days 8 and 21 when discouragement sets in. The second occurs between days 22 and 42, as the brain releases old patterns of behavior.[2]

Capturing the vision of our life and goals in written form can keep us focused and inspire us. This can help us keep our eye on the prize—hope for the future and the bright path ahead. It doesn't matter how we set our goals. It can be an elaborately decorated vision board or simple handwritten piece of paper, writing it down, planning it out, taking the first step, is important to healing after trauma. You can do it!

Activities

1. Imagine being ninety years old – what was your life story?
2. Create a vision board.
3. Set one SMART goal you can accomplish this week.

Sources

1 Leonard, K., & Watts, R. (2024, July 9). *The ultimate guide to S.M.A.R.T. goals.* Forbes Advisor. https://www.forbes.com/advisor/business/smart-goals/

2 Isabel, C.(2024, Aug 29). *The neuroscience of habits, how behavioral change rewires your brain.* The Mind, Brain, Body, Digest. https://blog.mindbrainbodylab.com/p/the-neuroscience-of-habits

CHAPTER 21

HEALING ENVIRONMENT

This Feels Like Home

I like to walk about amidst the beautiful things that adorn the world.

— George Santayana

My introduction to the concept of the healing environment came through a post-graduate certification program in *Global Health: Trauma and Recovery* with *Harvard Medical School*. Dr. Richard Mollica, a professor of psychiatry and director of the *Harvard Program in Refugee Trauma* (HPRT), is a leading expert in trauma recovery, particularly among refugees.[1] His pioneering research on restorative environments was a key a part of the course, focusing on designing and creating spaces that support trauma recovery. Dr. Mollica shared compelling studies demonstrating how our surroundings profoundly influence the healing process. He emphasized that "there is no healing without beauty," a principle applies to any setting—whether a tent in a refugee camp, a mansion, a doctor's office, or a government building.[2]

I never expected that his insights would soon become deeply personal. The timing was providential—the Harvard certification concluded only a few weeks before my trauma *Storm*. With these principles freshly in my mind, I focused on applying the concepts of an optimal healing environment to my journey, implementing them in my home, office, and car.[3]

According to my class notes, Dr. Mollica teaches that we are not immune to the influences of our habitat. He highlights the research of Whittemore et al. (2001), that "Guiding the Healing Environment is a philosophy of caring... the desire to develop a space that engenders feelings of peace, hope, upliftment, joy, reflection, and solace... opportunities for relaxation, enrichment, spiritual connection, humor, and play." This philosophy is rooted in the research-supported belief that these factors significantly impact the physical, emotional, and spiritual healing process.[4] Incorporating nature into our surroundings and decluttering our environment are key to creating a peaceful space for our body and mind to heal.

Realizing how important it was to pause in each space—like my home, office, and automobile—to reflect on how my body reacted and what I sensed, I began asking myself two main questions:

- *Does this space provide peace and joy?*
- *Does anything in this space, or the space itself, create anxiety or any type of stressful feelings?*

Listening to my internal thoughts and feelings, and making note of things that needed to be changed, I began to replace certain stress-inducing wall hangings, furniture, and accessories with items that brought joy and peace. I integrated natural elements like wood, stone, and beautiful plants to transform my surroundings, which took a little time. While some may need silence in their space, peaceful music helped create an environment I thrived in. With each change, certain areas of my habitat needed to be decluttered or refined. Dr. Mollica stresses the enormous benefits of restorative environments and notes that even the origin of the word *habitat* stems from the Latin verb *habitare* meaning "the total environment of a person or organism."[5]

Finding a Healing and Restorative Environment Through Nature

Natural elements incorporated into our environment not only increase human productivity in a work setting but also boost student test scores. Everyone feels better when the world around us is full of life and natural elements. In a study on human spaces, human creativity and perceived well-being increased by 15% through contact with natural elements, including natural sunlight, living flora, and water features in the indoor environment.

This concept was first described by American biologist Edward Wilson, who proposed that humans need to be affiliated with the natural world. Using the root *bio,* which means life, and the suffix *philic,* which means love, Wilson coined the term *biophilic design* to refer to constructed environments that reflect nature. Biophilic design reduces stress as it appeals to the human senses of sight, hearing, touch, and smell. Connections with natural elements improve emotional well-being and cognitive function and have overall positive effects on human health.[6]

In my home and office, I have added easy-to-care for plants, picture frames with natural wood elements, and artwork that not only features nature, but also has a calming effect on me. I also brought in some woven baskets and my favorite stone—a uniquely beautiful amethyst. Whether at home or in my office, I love the welcoming, naturally calming feel of my environment, and some clients have mentioned they appreciate the soothing atmosphere of my office space.

Indoor, Low Maintenance Natural Elements:

- **Plants:** succulents, cactus, bamboo, bonsai, peace lily, baby rubber plant, snake plant, money tree, prayer plant, ferns
- **Natural Elements:** gemstones, minerals, crystals, rocks, pebbles, wood, bamboo, rattan, cane, straw, hemp or jute
- **Natural Textures:** wool, cotton, wood
- **Natural light:** open curtains or blinds, with window film for privacy, allowing natural light in; build or install skylights or transom windows; circadian lighting systems; light wells
- **Scents:** dried flowers, fresh herbs, candles, cedar, sandalwood, pine, cinnamon, cloves, citrus peels
- **Water Features:** indoor water fountains, fishbowl, fish tanks

Additional elements to consider:

- Colors that bring joy and peace

- Comfortable furniture that feels inviting
- Textures that feel good to your senses
- Music sources

Healing and Self-Care Through Decluttering

The human mind has interesting ways of protecting itself. Clutter and chaos can be connected to feelings of trauma, so it makes sense that removing clutter is a healing action. By itself, clutter does not indicate trauma. Decluttering is a primary step when creating a healing environment. While decluttering, organizing, and cleaning are independent tasks, decluttering serves as a foundation, making cleaning and organizing more manageable.[7]

Always an organizer, one year during high school I asked for a filing cabinet for Christmas. My body and mind are calmer and less stressed when I am in a clean, well-organized space. Friends and family know my refrigerator is organized, my cupboards are neat, and my bins are labeled—which brings me joy. However, when creating a healing environment, I found more to declutter, which helped me feel grounded and at peace. After my traumatic experience, decluttering became even more essential, as my brain needed fewer distractions and less to think about and process.

I recognize that organizational skills come easier to some than to others, but be assured that there are great resources available to assist in organization endeavors. Organization, like other skills and talents, can be learned. A favorite show I enjoyed binge-watching during the 2020 COVID-19 shutdown, *Get Organized with the Home Edit* on Netflix, helped celebrities create, declutter, and organize. As humans, we are always learning. Inspiration can arise from seeing or reading how others declutter and organize spaces.

In 2014, Marie Kondo's passion for decluttering and organizing gained global recognition when her book *The Life-Changing Magic of Tidying Up: The Japanese Art of Decluttering,* was published in the United States. It has now been published in 44 countries. In 2019, she had her own Netflix series, *Tidying Up with Marie Kondo.* Marie's KonMari philosophies and simple methods of decluttering and organizing resonated with people worldwide: "To determine [if an object should be kept or discarded] when tidying, the key is to pick up each object one at a time, and ask yourself quietly, 'Does this spark joy?'"[8] Regardless of whether you want to ask if an item sparks joy, paying attention to how your body responds can be a big help in determining what to keep as you are changing your environment to one of peace. You might prefer asking, "Does this item bring me peace?" According to the KonMari philosophy's sixth rule of tidying, "Pay attention to how your body responds. Joy is personal, so everyone will experience it differently; Marie describes it as 'a little thrill,' as if the cells in your body are slowly rising." Through the process of selecting only those things that inspire joy, you can identify precisely what you love and what you need.[9]

One of my dream jobs would be working with a client on trauma therapy while simultaneously helping them declutter their homes and schedules, as the comprehensive package could be life-changing. We know that clutter impacts mental health. Peter Walsh, another professional declutterer and organizer, reminds us, "Clutter isn't just the stuff on the floor. It's anything that stands in the way of people living their best life."[10] There is something to be said about having a clean and organized work or living space. A *Princeton University* study discovered how the environment can impact our ability to complete tasks. It also affects our overall mental health, both positively and negatively.[11] If the physical environment feels scattered, our mental space will likely feel the same. Another study by the *University of Connecticut* demonstrated that eliminating clutter directly reduces stress, resulting in feeling happier, less anxious, and more confident.[12]

A 2019 *New York Times* article also highlighted a 2010 study showing that clutter negatively impacts overall mental well-being, especially in women, while also increasing:

- *Cortisol levels (stress hormones)*
- *Life dissatisfaction*
- *Procrastination*

These studies collectively demonstrate the profound impact that our environment—specifically clutter—can have on our mental health and overall well-being. Clutter literally and figuratively becomes a roadblock to decisions, happiness, success, and good health.[13]

Decluttering doesn't have to be done all at once. It can be approached one small space at a time. For instance, start with a drawer that feels stressful when you open it. Remove the items that make you feel stressed. Wipe it out and return the items that bring you peace. Now, there you go! You've created a healthier space. Great job!

You might clean off a shelf that has too many items. Donate clothes from your closet you haven't worn in a while. Empty garbage cans, do anything that makes you feel better about your space. Remember, the goal is to pay attention to how your body feels in your space and assess if the space is increasing your cortisol stress hormone or if your body feels at peace.

Major Changes

When assessing a healing environment after trauma, it may become clear to some that a space is tied too closely to a traumatic experience. For example, a home after a death or relationship breakup, or a car involved in an accident may still trigger anxiety. Your office space may feel claustrophobic. In these cases, an individual may need to decide whether the next step to creating a healing environment is to move to a new home, replace the car, or make other changes related to your environment.

Creating a healing environment is a life-long process as we maintain our spaces. However, once implemented, it can provide a space where the body can relax and feel at peace. It is a process worth investing in for healing and peace.

Activities

1. Find a drawer, shelf, or space to declutter.
2. Identify a space as your 'healing space' and bring in items that give you peace and joy.
3. Watch an organizing show for inspiration and ideas.

Additional Resources

- challengingdisorganization.org
- mariekondo.com
- declutterhub.com/peter-walsh/

Sources

1 Yanks, L. (n.d.). *'Applied religion': M.D. alum pioneers care for traumatized refugees.* Yale Divinity School. https://divinity.yale.edu/news/applied-religion-md-alum-pioneers-care-traumatized-refugees

2 Mass General Research Institute. (n.d.). *Richard Mollica, M.D. | Mass General Research Institute.* Retrieved January 15, 2025, from https://researchers.mgh.harvard.edu/profile/14158853/Richard-Mollica

3 Sakallaris, B. R., Macallister, L., Voss, M., Smith, K., & Jonas, W. B. (2015). Optimal healing environments. *Global Advances in Health and Medicine, 4*(3), 40–45. https://doi.org/10.7453/gahmj.2015.043

4 Anderson, K. (April 2001). *Personal class notes.*

5 American University of Beirut. (2016, October 6). *The new H5 model, trauma and recovery [Video]. YouTube. https://www.youtube.com/watch?v=Sg4oDzutqt8*

6 Kinnarps. (2023, May 10). *Design with nature to improve well-being. Kinnarps. https://www.kinnarps.us/knowledge/design-with-nature-to-improve-well-being/*

7 Buchanan, R. (2024, April 17). *Clutter and trauma: Here's how to start decluttering through it. Nourishing Minimalism. https://nourishingminimalism.com/clutter-trauma-decluttering/*

8 Kondo, M. (2014). *The Life-Changing Magic of Tidying up: The Japanese Art of Decluttering and Organizing. Ten Speed Press. pp.41-42.*

9 KonMari. (2021, November 3). Rule 6: *Ask yourself if it sparks joy. KonMari | the Official Website of Marie Kondo. https://konmari.com/marie-kondo-rules-of-tidying-sparks-joy*

10 Fielden, R. (2025, January 6). *Episode 270 – Peter Walsh: The Power of Clutter and its hold on us. The Declutter Hub. https://declutterhub.com/peter-walsh/*

11 Utah State University. (2023b, December 14). *The mental health benefits of decluttering.* USU. https://extension.usu.edu/mentalhealth/articles/the-mental-benefits-of-decluttering

12 Utah State University. (2023b, December 14). *The mental health benefits of decluttering.* USU. https://extension.usu.edu/mentalhealth/articles/the-mental-benefits-of-decluttering

13 Le Beau Lucchesi, E. (2019, January). *The unbearable heaviness of clutter. The New York Times. https://www.nytimes.com/2019/01/03/well/mind/clutter-stress-procrastination-psychology.html*

CHAPTER 22

JOURNALING

Pick Up Your Pen

When I look back on my personal story through my journals, it struck me my words had an unmatched power to heal me. To change me.

— Sandra Marinella

Emotions penned into expressive words are powerful. At times, I have a hard time holding back tears as I hear clients read their deepest emotions detailed in the pages of their journals. Even when I hear my clients discuss their trauma experiences, there is a depth and vulnerability that comes through written words. Sometimes, my clients are in awe as they witness their story take form through their writing.

When I reread my journal entries from the trauma *Storm Phase,* I feel sad for the girl who endured that kind of pain; it hurts my heart. Yet, I can also see how brave I was and how much I have healed. I am proud of the hard work I have put in to heal and can see how my story has unfolded through my writing. The pages also reveal the blessings and growth within my story.

Sometimes, reading my journal reminds me of moments I had forgotten, but also validates events that did occur that my brain might question. Keeping a journal expands our memory and helps us hold on to important moments. After trauma, writing may seem like some version of bleeding onto a page.[1] Journal writing doesn't have to be a formal process. Some of my entries came from texts to family, friends, emails I sent and even quick notes in my phone. I captured thoughts, feelings, and experiences in real time—in my car, at church, in a waiting room, or on an airplane.

Benefits of writing down our emotions and thoughts:

- Organizes our thoughts and feelings
- Eliminates the need to filter what we want to say
- Helps the brain sort through details of complex events
- Structures information in sequential order, creating a story
- Assigns specific words to our emotions and labeling them
- Creates a history of our experience
- Provides an outside perspective on our story
- Externalizes emotions for healthier processing

Improve Your Health

Over the past 25 years, a growing body of research has demonstrated the beneficial effects that writing about traumatic or stressful events has on physical and emotional health.[2] The physiological process involves the amygdala — a small part of your brain that is always on patrol for danger and can flood the body with hormones to help protect us. This can induce anxiety, panic, or any number of emotions that serve to protect us, but can be overzealous. Writing is much like shining a light into the unknown, helping us to calm down. There is wisdom in the saying, "*To name it is to tame it.*" As journaling becomes a habit, our amygdala no longer has to send alarms to the rest of our body, allowing us to regain a sense of calm, neutralizing unnecessary panic. Journaling gives us the opportunity to identify, process and categorize complex emotions and lessen their intensity.[3] Keeping a journal can help us transition through the *Trauma Impact Phases — Storm, Clearing* and finally to the *Sunshine Phase.*

Journaling about thoughts and emotions has many benefits. One study found more post-traumatic growth, better relationships, and a greater sense of strength, appreciation for life, and new possibilities for the future among participants who journaled. Not only that, writing specifically boosts our immune system.[4] A benefit we especially need in the face of pandemics! Anne Frank perfectly captured this when she wrote, "When I write, I can shake off all my cares. My sorrows disappear, my spirits are revived!"[5]

Activities

1. Pick up your pen. There are many ways to capture our feelings. Experiment and find your favorite way to journal.
    - App on a phone
    - Typing on a computer
    - Traditional journal
    - Notebook
    - Regular piece of paper
    - Journal with prompts
    - Decorate journal with a personal touch to reflect your identity
    - Express your feelings and events, with drawings instead of words
2. Is there a part of your journal you would like to share with someone in your circle or with a therapist?
3. Read old journal entries to see how your story has unfolded.

Sources

1 1956 June 17, Augusta Chronicle, Week in Review by John Harper, Page 2, Column 4, Augusta, Georgia. (GenealogyBank).

2 University of Wisconsin Integrative Health. (n.d.). Therapeutic journaling. In University of Wisconsin Integrative Health. https://www.fammed.wisc.edu/files/webfm-uploads/documents/outreach/im/tool-therapeutic-journaling.pdf

3 Malik, I. (2024, November 27). Proven benefits of journaling for stress relief and mental health. Our Mental Health. https://www.ourmental.health/stress-management/unlock-stress-relief-the-proven-power-of-journaling-for-mental-well-being

4 Newman, K. (2021). *How journaling can help you in Hard times.* Greater Good. https://greatergood.berkeley.edu/article/item/how_journaling_can_help_you_in_hard_times

5 Frank, A. (1996). *The Diary of a young girl: The Definitive Edition.* Vintage. p. 251.

CHAPTER 23

LAUGHTER & FUN

The Best Medicines

Laughter rises out of tragedy when you need it the most and rewards you for your courage.

— Erma Bombeck

Laughter and fun are some of the most powerful tools for healing from trauma. They can distract us from our sadness, help us forget about life challenges, and offer moments of connection with joy. Laughter strengthens our social bonds and helps us to feel better. As the saying goes, "Laughter is the best medicine," but it's even more than medicine. It strengthens our lungs and heart, reduces pain, and reduces stress.[1] When we are in the healing process, having fun may not seem like a priority, but it is necessary! At times, we may feel like we will never laugh and have fun the way we used to. Even I felt that way. Can laughing and having fun become effortless again? The answer is yes!

Psychologist Taylor Hartman developed *The Color Profile,* (also called *The People Profile*) to explain core personality motivations. It links color to our core motivations of red (power), white (peace), blue (intimacy), or yellow (fun). While individuals can have traits from multiple colors, it was no surprise that mine is a yellow oriented personality —fun—as it is my dominant motivation. "Yellows love to have fun. The joy of living in the moment and doing something just for the sake of doing it is the driving force for these people. Yellows offer the gifts of enthusiasm and optimism. They are generally charismatic, spontaneous, and sociable."[2] The test confirmed what I knew. I craved a life filled with fun and laughter.

Anything we do should be sprinkled with fun. It makes life more enjoyable. My kids still talk about how even chores were fun when I created the "Superman game". We wrote various chores on slips of paper and put them in a bowl, then added in other slips of paper that had fun and creative activities. We would take turns pulling out a piece of paper, not knowing what the next activity would be. As we pulled out the slip of paper, my four kids and I rushed to do that activity. We bounced from cleaning the bathroom sink to having a five-minute dance party, vacuuming to running laps around the house, dusting to a sock-throwing war, mopping the kitchen floor to doing somersaults. Chores became exciting and we made great memories. I loved it!

Trauma can undermine our personality, muting or erasing what once felt natural. Before my trauma, laughter and fun were effortless. Afterward, it felt forced, disconnected, and anything but natural. It was as if a core piece of me had died. I know this is a real feeling for those going through trauma. It can feel difficult to imagine a day when fun and laughter will take center stage again—but it can happen.

The saying "keep on keepin' on" rings true in the healing process. What felt natural will eventually return. Being surrounded by friends and family who have a great sense of humor helped lift my spirits. During the healing process, I made intentional efforts to embrace opportunities for fun and humor in my life. I recommend intentionally surrounding yourself with your favorite people. Watching a show with a friend or loved one remembering funny events in the past are ways to increase the "feel good" neurotransmitters like dopamine, serotonin, and an array of other happy, healthy endorphins.[3]

Our bodies thrive, grow, and heal when we are happy. Even planning to enjoy an activity has a positive effect. "One study found that people who just thought about watching their favorite movie actually raised their endorphin levels by 27 percent."[4] During trauma, remembering what once brought laughter and joy is part of the healing process as you move through the *Trauma Impact Phases*. Perhaps a spark of excitement and fun comes with the thought of exploring a new activity or revisiting a past hobby.

One man, who had been very ill and nearly died, had limited strength. Dressing, standing, and eating drained all his energy. Moving required great effort. He was depressed and discouraged because of the loss of his health. His family intentionally found silly movies for him to watch. His laughter was a gift, and it was healing. I want you to know that your laughter will help you heal.

Laughter can boost energy, relieve stress, and reduce depression. The energy we gain from laughter is remarkable.[5] During the *Clearing* and *Sunshine Phases,* I intentionally sought fun out. I tried it all — amusement parks, comedy clubs, plays, movies, concerts, karaoke, figure skating lessons, pickleball, and even a little thrill seeking to challenge my fear of heights. My adrenaline was pushed to the limits when I went on the sky coaster at Lagoon Amusement Park in Utah. It pulls you up 150 feet before dropping you towards the ground, reaching speeds of 80 mph as you swing back and forth in the air like Superman. It was exhilarating and made me feel alive—and of course, made me laugh with excitement.

Actor Matt LeBlanc, who starred in the TV show *Friends,* said it best: "I believe that laughter is the best emotional Band-Aid in the world. It's like nature's Neosporin."[6] Our body does have the power to heal us, and laughter is proof of that!

Activities

1. Make a list of five fun things you can do within the next ten days. Then try to do them!
2. Make a list of movies, books, or media that make you laugh. Watch or read at least 2 this week.
3. Take this fun personality test: https://taylorhartman.com/assessment-information

Sources

1 Finlay, L. (2024, March 1). 8 health benefits of laughing, according to neuroscience research. The Healthy. https://www.thehealthy.com/habits/health-benefits-of-laughter/.

2 *Assessment Information - Color code Personality Assessment - TaylorHartman.* (2024, February 6). TaylorHartman. https://taylorhartman.com/assessment-information/

3 Edwards, S. (2011, December 19). Humor, laughter, and those aha moments. Harvard Medical School. https://hms.harvard.edu/news/humor-laughter-those-aha-moments

4 Achor, S. (2018). The happiness advantage: How a Positive Brain Fuels Success in Work and Life. Crown Currency. p. 52.

5 Hayme Salomone Home (2022, August 18). Four health benefits of fun: Heal your mind and body. Haym Salomon Home for Nursing & Rehabilitation. https://www.haymsalomonhome.com/four-health-benefits-of-fun/

6 Maan, M. (2021, July 26). 10 Most Famous Quotes by FRIENDS star, Matt LeBlanc. Epic Quotes. https://www.epicquotes.com/10-most-famous-quotes-by-friends-star-matt-leblanc/

CHAPTER 24

MEDICATION

What Should I Do?

The purpose of a doctor is to increase the quality of life.

— Adapted from Patch Adams

Medications used for trauma symptoms such as anxiety, depression, mood disorders, and sleep disturbances can be an effective resource, especially when combined with other resources like mental health counseling. When it comes to depression, a meta-analysis of 25 studies showed that a combination of medication and therapy provides more relief than only using medication.[1]

Through my traumatic experience and recovery, I was usually able to manage my symptoms through a variety of interventions outside of medication, but during the *Storm Phase,* I needed to take an anti-anxiety medication to help my brain calm down, allowing me to sleep and eat. Thankfully, the medication was effective in reducing my symptoms so I could function in my daily life. Once I entered the *Clearing Phase* feeling more in control, I was able to wean off the medication as I began applying a variety of interventions, including therapy. During the *Clearing Phase,* when my anxiety was triggered, I was able to reduce symptoms by taking over-the-counter supplements that had calming effects and assisted with sleeping. Even though I was able to phase out medications during the *Clearing Phase,* please note that some people may need to stay on medications long-term due to how their body functions. It is critical for everyone to listen to their bodies and follow up with their medical doctor and mental health therapist to create an effective treatment plan.

While working with clients, I have observed a significant reduction in symptoms when clients have partnered with their primary care physician or psychiatrist to find an effective medication. Medications used to treat anxiety, depression, and other mental health issues are called psychotropic medications. They work by changing chemical levels and adjusting neurotransmitters in the brain.[2] Medications work differently for every individual, so be patient while finding the medication that works for your body.

The following are common types of medications prescribed to reduce symptoms associated with a trauma response:

- **Anti-depressant:** Used to treat moderate to severe depression, anxiety disorders, and eating disorders
- **Anti-anxiety:** Used to help you feel calmer or allow you to sleep
- **Anti-psychotic:** Used to treat schizophrenia, schizoaffective disorder, psychosis, and sometimes severe anxiety or bipolar disorder
- **Mood stabilizers:** Used to help you avoid extreme mood swings, and may be prescribed for bipolar disorder
- **Tranquilizers and sleeping pills:** Used to reduce anxiety and insomnia, but are usually only used briefly because longer use can cause dependency

Views on psychotropic medications can vary. Some people prefer holistic approaches, have concerns about misuse, or are worried about potential side effects. These concerns are valid, but it is undeniable that when needed, that psychotropic medications can be effective in reducing or alleviating symptoms of mental health conditions. It is essential to work with medical professionals and become an educated consumer when deciding if this is an intervention tool that could assist in your healing and recovery process.

Activities

1. Research and discuss with a health professional regarding over-the-counter medications that could reduce symptoms.
2. Discuss potential prescription medications with your medical provider.
3. If you have been on medications for a while, assess and discuss with your medical provider the goals of longevity. Is it possible to phase off the medication(s) once other interventions and coping tools are in place?

Sources

1 Harvard Health. (2020, May 26). *Medication or therapy for depression? Or both?* https://www.health.harvard.edu/staying-healthy/medication-or-therapy-for-depression-or-both

2 Ghoshal, M. (2024, August 29). *What is a psychotropic drug?* Healthline. https://www.healthline.com/health/what-is-a-psychotropic-drug#Why-are-psychotropic-drugs-prescribed

CHAPTER 25

MINDFULNESS

Just Relax and Breathe

Meditation is a vital way to purify and quiet the mind, thus rejuvenating the body.

— Deepak Chopra

Yoga, breathing techniques, and mindfulness exercises have become more popular in recent years due to increased recognition of the benefits to mind and body. Researchers have recently emphasized the growing body of evidence showing that yoga can be an effective treatment for various mental health conditions.[1] Support is growing for these practices as effective mental health therapies.

If this book had been written even five years earlier, I might be writing a different narrative as I wasn't completely convinced of the benefits of these interventions. I would have categorized them as "frou-frou," meaning I thought they weren't stable and effective tools. I was wrong, and my opinion has been changed by personal experience. Yoga, breathing techniques, and mindfulness are very effective therapeutic tools in recovery and support grounding of the body and mind. In fact, I believe they are essential and foundational to mental health balance and healing.

Over the years, friends and family have encouraged or highly advocated for mindful interventions. Of course, I knew the philosophy around yoga and mindfulness had been around for centuries so there must be something to it, but I still wasn't a believer. I had convinced myself that if I was going to spend an hour on an activity dedicated to my body, it would be more beneficial to do an activity that was more active and intense. My past experience with yoga from more than a decade before did not feel like a "good workout" and frankly, I was bored and unable to see the benefits.

After my trauma *Storm* though, I was willing to experiment with these methods again. Studies have shown how yoga, breathing techniques, and mindfulness can calm the body and mind, and my body was in a constant state of anxiety and trauma response. So, I began my journey and enrolled in a hot yoga class with my daughter.

Yoga

During my first class, I felt completely awkward, and it became apparent that I had much to improve in terms of my balance and keeping my mind focused. Others in the class seemed like they flowed with grace and perfect balance, and I felt like I was flailing around and had to lay down for the second half of the class due to exhaustion. Even though I felt out of place, awkward, and a bit like a failure, I surprisingly felt more relaxed and even felt an openness within my body. A sense of relief and calmness settled over me and my stress level decreased. I felt at peace and could even feel a sense of connection with my body and mind, which helped me feel empowered. As I intentionally focused on my breathing, my anxiety and fears were calming. Even though I felt like an awkward duck in the middle of swans during that first class, I wanted to continue showing up for classes to capture the benefits it could offer.

I have been attending yoga classes for several years now and still have awkward moments and, like any skill, there is always more to learn. Nevertheless, my balance has improved, and the terminology no longer seems like a foreign language. Words and phrases such as Warrior One, Namaste, Tree Pose, and Vinyasa make sense to me now. Yoga is an assessment tool that helps me to gauge my physical strength and balance, along with understanding the state of my mind regarding stillness of mind and focus. As I enter the class, I find an area of my life I need to let go of to find peace or an area to focus on to bring empowerment and positive energy.

Yoga is a tool that helps us stay connected and aware of our thoughts, feelings, and emotions, which in turn helps us center on what we would like to think in our hearts. Listening to your heart is a great skill. Depending on how I am feeling, I try to select a class that challenges me physically with endurance, strength, balance, and deep stretching. Other times, I choose a class focused on meditation and calm. These classes might incorporate lighted candles and calming music that helps to soothe my mind and releases tension in my body. There are also classes that incorporate sound vibrations, called sound baths, which use sound waves to promote relaxation and emotional release. The first time I experienced a sound bath was when I attended a yoga class with my daughter. We were astonished when, during a specific sound wave, tears unexpectedly began to pour down our faces. The sound released emotions we did not anticipate. It was a singular experience that felt cleansing.

There are various types of yoga classes. I personally love attending hot yoga as the heat seems to help my muscles with the deep stretches and soothes my arthritis. At times I feel like I am going to die and melt away in the 100-degree humid sauna, but I love how my body feels when I am done. Of course, others would hate the heat! Each person needs to find the type of yoga that works best for their body and mind.

If cost is a concern, look for community classes that are more affordable. The beauty of yoga is it is self-paced and people of any age, size, or ability can join in. It is an individual journey and just showing up and doing your best counts! Yoga can also be practiced at home using various online resources, which provide step-by-step guidance through each pose.

The benefits are worth the effort because as Dr. Natalie Nevins explains, "Regular yoga practice creates mental clarity and calmness; increases body awareness; relieves chronic stress patterns; relaxes the mind; centers attention; and sharpens concentration."[2]

Research has proven practicing yoga is beneficial, particularly in addressing symptoms of depression and post-traumatic stress disorder (PTSD).[3] If you're not already, perhaps one day soon you will embrace yoga too!

Meditation

Mindfulness is about teaching the mind and body to be present in the moment and to have full awareness of your thoughts, breathing, and body. It can take practice, but with each session, you will be one step closer to having more control of your mind and body in order to create stillness. For beginners, a good starting point is to meditate for 5-10 minutes at least 3 times a week, gradually increasing the time to at least 15-20 minutes a day.[4] With all that needs to be done in a day, this might seem challenging, so do what you can. Remember, any time spent on meditation is beneficial.

In a fascinating study, neuroscientists found that monks who made meditation a regular lifelong practice saw growth in their left prefrontal cortex—a part of the brain that helps regulate happiness and mood. Meditation feels foreign and strange to many people, but it can have enormous benefits even in only a few minutes a day. After meditating, we feel calm and content and are more aware of ourselves and our surroundings. We even feel more empathy. And, like the monks helped prove, making meditation a regular practice can permanently rewire the brain, increasing our happiness and even improving immune system function. The bottom line? Meditation can help us be healthier and happier.[5]

Harvard Health offers the two following meditation exercises that are perfect for beginners wanting to give it a try:

A Meditation Exercise

This exercise teaches basic mindfulness meditation:

1. Sit on a straight-backed chair or cross-legged on the floor
2. Focus on an aspect of your breathing, such as the sensations of air flowing into your nostrils and out of your mouth, or your belly rising and falling as you inhale and exhale
3. Once you've narrowed your concentration in this way, begin to widen your focus. Become aware of sounds, sensations, and ideas

4. Embrace and consider each thought or sensation without judging it good or bad. If your mind starts to race, re-turn your focus to your breathing. Then expand your awareness again[6]

The benefits of mindfulness meditation increase with consistent practice. Like any skill, the more you do, the greater the benefits and the easier it becomes. That said, even brief sessions can be effective. No matter the duration, any amount of meditation can have positive results.

Practicing Awareness In Daily Life

A less formal approach to mindfulness can also help you stay in the present and fully participate in your life. You can choose any task or moment to practice informal mindfulness, whether eating, showering, walking or interacting with a loved one.

An informal exercise:

1. Start by bringing your attention to the sensations in your body
2. Breathe in through your nose, allowing the air to fill your lungs. Let your abdomen expand fully. Then breathe out slowly through your mouth. This pattern may slow down your heart rate and lower your blood pressure, helping you relax. Notice the sensations of each inhalation and exhalation
3. Proceed with the task at hand slowly and with full deliberation
4. Engage your senses fully. Notice each sight, touch, and sound so that you savor every sensation
5. When you notice that your mind has wandered from the task at hand, gently bring your attention back to the sensations of the moment[7]

Breathing

Breathing exercises are beneficial in calming the body and reducing stress. Changes in breathing are a very normal part of a trauma response. If you feel anxious, you will likely find yourself taking short, shallow breaths and using your shoulders instead of your diaphragm to breathe deeply.[8]

Breathing exercises are an effective tool for calming the nervous system during times of anxiety, stress, or emotional dysregulation. There are a variety of breathing exercises that can be learned through online resources or a phone app. One of the most popular breathing exercises that is easy to engage in wherever you are is called 4-7-8. The 4-7-8 breathing technique is when you inhale for 4 seconds, hold your breath for 7 seconds, then slowly exhale for 8 seconds.[9]

Recovering from trauma can open opportunities to learn new skills that are beneficial not only for your trauma recovery but for lifelong mental and physical health. Yoga, mindfulness exercises, and breathing activities can contribute to overall wellness.

"Namaste" is a term used in yoga when parting ways and means, "The divine light within me salutes the divine light within you."[10]

Namaste, and I wish you well on your journey.

Activities

1. Attend a yoga class in person or find a program online.
2. Practice the breathing and meditation exercises described in this chapter.
3. Find a sound bath in your community to try.

Sources

1 Nyer, M., Nauphal, M., Roberg, R., & Streeter, C. (2018). Applications of Yoga in Psychiatry: What We Know. *American Psychiatric Publication, 1:12-18,* Epub 2018 Jan 24. PMID: 31975895; PMCID: PMC6519580. https://doi.org/10.1176/appi.focus.20170055

2 *Benefits of yoga | American Osteopathic Association. (2021, January 22). American Osteopathic Association. https://osteopathic.org/what-is-osteopathic-medicine/benefits-of-yoga*

3 Nyer, M., Nauphal, M., Roberg, R., & Streeter, C. (2018). Applications of Yoga in Psychiatry: What We Know. *American Psychiatric Publication, 1:12-18,* Epub 2018 Jan 24. PMID: 31975895; PMCID: PMC6519580. https://doi.org/10.1176/appi.focus.20170055

4 Calm. (n.d.). *How often should I meditate: Here's what you need to know. Calm. Retrieved February 5, 2025, from https://www.calm.com/blog/how-often-should-i-meditate*

5 Achor, S. (2018). *The happiness advantage: How a Positive Brain Fuels Success in Work and Life.* Crown Currency. p.52

6 Harvard Health. (2021, March 17). *Two mindfulness meditation exercises to try.* https://www.health.harvard.edu/alternative-and-integrative-health/two-mindfulness-meditation-exercises-to-try

7 Harvard Health. (2021, March 17). Two mindfulness meditation exercises to try. https://www.health.harvard.edu/alternative-and-integrative-health/two-mindfulness-meditation-exercises-to-try

8 Department of Health & Human Services. (n.d.). *Breathing to reduce stress.* Better Health Channel. https://www.betterhealth.vic.gov.au/health/healthyliving/breathing-to-reduce-stress

9 Cronkleton, E. (2024, May 17). *10 breathing exercises to try when you're feeling stressed.* Healthline. https://www.healthline.com/health/breathing-exercise#faq

10 McLean Meditation Institute & the Meditation Teacher Academy. (2025, February 4). *Glossary of Yoga & Meditation Terms - McLean Meditation Institute.* McLean Meditation Institute - Meditation & Mindfulness Teacher Academy. https://mcleanmeditation.com/glossary-of-terms

CHAPTER 26

MOTIVATIONAL MESSAGING

Let's Do This!

Nobody can go back and start a new beginning,
but anyone can start today and make a new ending.

— Maria Robinson

Soon after my traumatic experience, I knew I had to start putting down solid anchors to help ground me so I wouldn't be swept away by feelings of darkness and a desire to "dissolve" and "be nothing." I wanted to fight against the weight of the chains of trauma pulling me into the black hole of worthlessness and negative beliefs, so I had to be intentional in my thoughts and actions. One of the first intentional activities I did was to write a positive and motivational message on my bathroom mirror that I could see multiple times a day. Of course, with my great love of music, I found this message in a song. Breaking it down, the lyrics became my motivational message, a foundation and a source of hope.

Trauma recovery is a battle, and my battle plan was to fight back with positive thoughts, plans, and messages. For thousands of years, battlefield drummers signaled commands and motivated troops to fight with courage, dignity, and unity.[1] My mirror message became my support signal for this battle.

The motivational messaging had five key parts. The first three came from the lyrics of "Say I Won't" by MercyMe. Listening to that song in combination with my new motivational message gave me courage, inspiration, dignity, and strength. I listened to it hundreds of times. The last two parts of my motivational messaging were from quotes I felt connected to. For each phrase, I added a picture that represents that message. This message as a whole held me during the darkest moments of the traumatic experience, and I would purposefully spend time reciting the following lines each time I was standing at my bathroom mirror.

"Today was the beginning of my new life."

Our lives look different after trauma, but it doesn't mean they have ended. The music video of "Say I Won't" by MercyMe, begins with the narrative of quadruple amputee Gary Miracle.[2] After a medical crisis, Gary lost all four of his limbs, making him a quadriplegic. His new life meant he had to relearn everything.[3] While most individuals will not experience the same challenges as Gary Miracle, trauma requires that we learn new ways to live our lives. Life will look and feel different from this moment on; there is no going back. I was on a significantly different path in how I would see myself and experience the world.

The image I chose for this line was my favorite happy flower—a daisy. The daisy reminded me of the fields in New Hampshire where I grew up, as I always loved seeing fields of wild daisies blooming. Even after the harshest winter, spring still comes and the world becomes beautiful, blooming again.

"I will live a meaningful life."

To me, life has a divine purpose, and I didn't want to merely exist. I wanted to live a meaningful life. Intentionally, I chose to live, grow, and evolve into the person I wanted to be and not let the trauma, with its new fears and insecurities, define me. I was going to determine my path forward. The picture of a phoenix rising was the image I chose for this section. The phoenix is a mythical bird that rises from the ashes of its predecessor to symbolize renewal, rebirth, and hope. I wanted to be like a phoenix.[4]

"I can do all things through Christ who strengthens me."

After my trauma, I needed to anchor my foundation, which is built on my belief in Jesus Christ. I find safety, strength and peace in my belief in Christ. I share my faith as an example of how it serves as a guide for me, knowing that each individual may find strength in their own beliefs. My co-writer and friend Teresa keeps a framed, 20-year old handwritten note from a friend who passed. It says "Tough times never last. Tough people do," followed by the verse quoted above, "I can do all things through Christ who strengthens me!"[5] The image I chose to go along with this quote is a picture of Jesus Christ with his hands reaching out to me.

"Don't put trust in others–put trust in yourself that you will be okay."

The purpose of this phrase was to empower me to put trust in myself. Unfortunately, trauma can stem from another's actions or words. Trusting others has been a lifelong struggle for me, as my traumas, even from a young age, were due to the choices of others.

If my memory serves me correctly, I learned about this concept by watching the *Dr. Phil* show sometime in the 1990s. Dr. Phil, a clinical and forensic psychologist, is best known as a TV personality.[6] In each episode, he engages with individuals, couples, and families who need assistance in navigating challenging life circumstances. The episode I remember dealt with a wife's extramarital affair. Assessing if the relationship was salvageable, the husband asked Dr. Phil how he could ever trust his wife again. Dr. Phil advised that we don't have to rely on others for trust—we can trust ourselves that we will be okay, even when others break that trust. This advice that we can rely on ourselves to be okay became a powerful reminder and a helpful motivation. I was able to take responsibility for myself, my feelings, my security and my future.

Age and wisdom prove that humans are imperfect and always evolving, for good or bad. To expect others to always show up safely and exactly how we need physically and emotionally is unrealistic. Along the way, the trust of others might be broken and injuries to our heart and soul can happen. Before watching this episode, I invested a lot of emotional energy hoping and praying that those closest to me would keep me safe and never hurt me. However, past trauma had already taught me that humans are imperfect. They can be abusive and neglectful, or leave without warning. So, due to past traumas, my body was always in a protective mode. What Dr. Phil's statement taught me is that I could shift from others holding the control of my trust to holding it within myself. This means that I can trust myself no matter how other people disappoint or impact me. Whatever happens, I have the power to be okay. I am not saying this is easy, especially right after trauma caused by another's actions, but it is foundationally a concept that I believe to be true and choose to fight for. For this section, I used the same picture I used for number five below.

"I am capable of doing hard things."

I knew in my soul that I could do hard things, but the darkness and heaviness of the trauma at times felt insurmountable. I felt so broken and weak, but knew I had to dig deep and give it all I had so the trauma did not consume me and determine my path and destination.

The picture I used to represent this motivational thought was an image of a beautiful broken bowl that had been repaired with gold powder using a 15th-century Japanese practice known as *kintsugi*, meaning "to join with gold." It is a reminder to stay optimistic when things fall apart and to celebrate the flaws and missteps of life: "[Kintsugi] not only teaches calm when a cherished piece of pottery breaks; it is a reminder of the beauty of human fragility as well." This tradition "highlights imperfections rather than hiding them."[7]

When you try to mend something such as a bowl, plate, or cup, it is challenging to get all the pieces to stay in place. It requires effort and sometimes multiple attempts, but I relied on the picture of the repaired bowl to keep in mind how beautiful it looks when finished. The bowls would not be as beautiful without the gold-filled cracks. When we pick up the pieces and start mending our lives after defeat, disappointment, heartbreak, regrets, disillusion, or failure, those cracks become gold-filled. They are emotionally expensive experiences, but the gold we use to repair ourselves retains value for the rest of our lives. I had to continue to believe that I could do hard things and write my own story and destiny.

Learning About Me

With the brokenness from trauma comes an opportunity to evaluate ourselves and grow into the type of person we want to be, but it takes conscious, intentional steps. In this journey of rediscovery, part of my growth was learning who I was and how others saw me, something I had lost touch with after the trauma *Storm*. In the book *Leveling Up* by Ryan Leak, he suggests asking questions to help us grow and develop. He writes, "For self-awareness to really blossom, you must do something difficult: go ask people what they think of you. Answering the question, "What is it like to be on the other side of me?"[8] I took the opportunity to ask about twenty of my family members and close friends, "What do you see as my talents and strengths?" and, "What do you see that I could improve on?" Genuinely open to learning from the responses, I was surprised at some of the answers regarding the talents and strengths people saw in me. I realized that the talents and strengths I could see in myself in the past, I didn't recognize as being part of me anymore. I questioned whether I would ever recognize them in myself again.

My good friends and family offered kind and hopeful feedback, which I sincerely appreciated for its honesty. I saw areas I could improve in and took those responses to heart as I saw truth in the loving messages. The feedback was another piece of rebuilding. I became intentional about including it in my purposeful growth to transform trauma into hope and healing.

Making it Personal

One woman went to college after a traumatic brain injury that affected her ability to read and perform math. As a somewhat private person, she did not want to ask for additional help. She had to relearn subjects that once came easily, but now they were unfamiliar and confusing. Her comprehension, ability to concentrate, and ability to retain information had changed. It was scary. Always afraid she would fail, she created a playlist that gave her courage when she felt the most fearful. One song became a singular favorite that she played on a loop: "Home" by Phillip Phillips.[9] The song's message about settling down and not giving into fear carried her all the way to graduation.

What you choose for your motivational message can be anything—a song, a poem, a story, a photograph, or even a single quote. You don't have to create five separate motivations with accompanying images as I did—but you can!

Activities

1. Create your own motivational message through creative ways, such as a drawing or making a collage.
2. What messages in songs, poems, books, or quotes speak to you and would be motivational phrases to read for inspiration and strength? Keep a list of them available to read.
3. Watch a movie, or look up a music video or YouTube segment that highlights a motivational and inspiring story. Write down the strengths that they have that you want to incorporate into your own life.

Sources

1 Fondation Napoleon. (2012, May 7). *Marching to the Drums: A history of military drums and drummers - Napoleon.org.* napoleon.org. https://www.napoleon.org/en/magazine/publications/marching-to-the-drums-a-history-of-military-drums-and-drummers/

2 MercyMeVEVO. (2020, December 4). *MercyMe - Say I Won't (Official Music Video)* [Video]. YouTube. https://www.youtube.com/watch?v=UhTHgaCjTJs

3 MercyMe. (2021, March 5). *The story of Gary Miracle* [Video]. YouTube. https://www.youtube.com/watch?v=R2GgWiVZa18

4 Geller, (2018, September 29). *Phoenix - Description, history and stories | Mythology.net.* Mythology.net. https://mythology.net/mythical-creatures/phoenix/

5 Philippians 4:13, KJV

6 About Dr.Phil | *Official Website | Dr. Phil.* (n.d.). https://www.drphil.com/about-dr-phil/

7 Sho, T. (2022, February 25). *Kintsugi: Japan's ancient art of embracing imperfection.* https://www.bbc.com/travel/article/20210107-kintsugi-japans-ancient-art-of-embracing-imperfection

8 Leak, R. (2024). *Leveling up: 12 Questions to Elevate Your Personal and Professional Development,* p.27

9 Phillip Phillips wins 'American Idol (2018, June 25). *Rolling Stone.*

CHAPTER 27

MUSIC

Healing Emotions Through Song

Music can heal the wounds which medicine cannot touch.

— Debasish Mridha

Out of the many tools available in overcoming trauma, connecting with our favorite music stands out as a clear winner. Music in all its forms and varieties is healing. Whether you are working to recover from trauma or know someone who is, music provides a special form of relief. This was true for me as I worked through my thoughts while listening to my recovery songs. Even when I felt sad and cried while processing my emotions, I could ground myself, and move forward. As a universal language, music can relieve suffering, lessen pain, and bring comfort to our souls.[1]

Music was a large part of my healing process. The utility, availability, and versatility of music are only some of the reasons it's so influential. We don't have to be professional musicians to make or enjoy music. No matter if we are a wannabe rock star in the shower or one who belts out all our emotions in our car, we can all enjoy music—whether it's playing a radio, creating a new playlist, or just humming a favorite tune. Music brings us together and transcends time. Hearing a familiar song can take us to another place and time.[2]

Music is a Necessity

Every tool discussed in this book engages the brain, releasing dopamine and endorphins. However, music is one of the most powerful and easily accessible tools. It transcends social, emotional, and language barriers, allowing us to communicate without words.[3] Recent research recognizes music as an effective therapy for overcoming mental health challenges such as loneliness, fear, and depression. The human brain can identify an entire melody from a single note. Listening to our favorite music or creating music ourselves stimulates neurons, increasing blood flow to several parts of the brain at once. Music engages all regions of the brain, modulates dopamine, and strengthens neurons, making us smarter, happier, and more resilient.[4] Moreover, listening to classically composed music such as Mozart, Brahms, or Beethoven improves the neuroplasticity of the brain, which is the brain's ability to reorganize its structure, strengthen neural networks, and increase our ability to learn and manage trauma.[5] Beloved author and neurologist Oliver Sacks, described as the "poet laureate of medicine" by the *New York Times,* once shared, "Music can lift us out of depression or move us to tears—it is a remedy, a tonic, orange juice for the ear. But for many of my neurological patients, music is even more—it can provide access, even when no medication can, to movement, to speech, to life. For them, music is not a luxury, but a necessity."[6]

Music held me during the most difficult times. A powerful therapeutic resource was my playlist titled "Recovery." This playlist holds songs relating to some of my deepest sorrows and intense pain, but also songs that give me strength and hope. Contemplating where I was emotionally compared with where I wanted to be, I intentionally selected songs that reflected some of my brokenness, along with the hope for healing, resilience, peace, and joy. Creating this list became a process of self-repair, as if each song was written just for me. I spent countless hours listening to this playlist while sitting in my car, driving, lying on my bed, taking a walk, or going on a hike or bike ride. As you walk through this journey with me, I invite you to spend some time creating your own music playlists. While we all love different genres of music, any music helps to remove feelings of isolation and loneliness. As the words or sounds of the artist reverberate with our emotions, our hearts and minds find solace. Music is a powerful tool. It evokes emotions, and the poetry in the music can put feelings into words. Some artists have been with me through some of my darkest days when nobody else was around. They, of course, do not know how profoundly they impacted me. Music is so powerful, I felt understood and supported through their lyrics and tunes. It is a healing gift.

In your healing journey, I encourage you to search for music that soothes your soul, gives you strength and courage, helps you fight depression, fills you with hope, and creates feelings of joy. The songs below were just a few of my favorites. Rachel Platten's songs were especially helpful with my feelings of anxiety and depression.

Kelli's "Recovery" Playlist

Stand Still
Noah Cyrus and Billy Ray Cyrus

Beauty in the Struggle
Bryan Martin and Craig Campbell

Brighter Side
The Satellite Station

You're Gonna Be Ok
Jenn Johnson

Mercy
Rachel Platten

Fight Song
Rachel Platten

Falls
Odesza and Sasha Alex Sloan

Breathe Out
Rob Thomas

Say I Won't
Mercy Me

Better Place
Rachel Platten

Bad Thoughts
Rachel Platten

Activities

1. Find a simple way to have music with you: a radio, YouTube, record player, or an app on a digital device.
2. Take the time to create playlists and name them something such as "Courage," "Recovery," "Hope," etc.
3. Spend some time listening to music that evokes happy memories from your past.

Sources

1 Cross, L. (2021). Utilizing music therapy to manage chronic pain. *www.medcentral.com*. Retrieved January 17, 2025, from https://www.medcentral.com/pain/alternative-therapies/utilizing-music-therapy-manage-chronic-pain

2 Kapur, S., Craik, F. I. M., Jones, C., Brown, G. M., Houle, S., & Tulving, E. (1995). Functional role of the prefrontal cortex in retrieval of memories: A PET study. *NeuroReport, 6*(14), 1880–1884. https://doi.org/10.1097/00001756-199510020-00019

3 TEDx Talks, & Wooten, V. (2013, May 30). *Music as a Language: Victor Wooten at TEDxGabriolaIsland* [Video]. YouTube. https://www.youtube.com/watch?v=2zvjW9arAZ0

4 ideacity & Levitin, D. (2020, July 28). *Daniel Levitin - Your Brain on Music* [Video]. YouTube. https://www.youtube.com/watch?v=lyt8EmsJIBA

5 Gamma, E. (2023, August 17). *Brain Plasticity in Psychology | Neuroplasticity*. Simply Psychology. https://www.simplypsychology.org/brain-plasticity.html

6 Cowles, Gregory (30 August 2015). "Oliver Sacks, Neurologist Who Wrote About the Brain's Quirks, Dies at 82". *The New York Times.* Archived from the original on 20 January 2021.--- or see *** *Oliver Sacks dies in New York aged 82.* (2015, August 30). BBC News. https://web.archive.org/web/20160927133718/http://www.bbc.co.uk/news/uk-34102119 Emphasis added.

CHAPTER 28

RETREATS

Take Me Away!

It is always our own self that we find at the end of the journey.

— Ella Maillart

Take me away! While in the depths of healing during the *Clearing Phase*, many people experience a need for a change to help break the trauma loop, as discussed in Chapter 15. I know that was true for me. I could feel it deep within me—an overwhelming, desperate craving for a therapeutic retreat. My body desired a calm, healing space that would provide quiet, peace, reflection, self-care, emotional support, and perhaps new adventures and joyful experiences. These, in addition to therapeutic interventions specific to trauma recovery, would create empowerment. The high anxiety in my body was screaming for some downtime and a healing retreat.

My clients and friends who have attended retreats report feeling rejuvenated and motivated after their experiences. A study sponsored by the non-profit Saprea, which offers retreats for women healing from the trauma of sexual abuse, found that "individuals who participated in the retreat intervention exhibited a significant decrease in PTSD. The study also showed an increase in life satisfaction, social support, and coping self-efficacy."[1] Retreats can be an effective therapeutic tool for advancing the healing process.

There were a few weeks at the start of my healing process when I would spend hours online looking at healing retreats around the world. Since my body was craving tropical climates and warmth, I was looking for a therapeutic retreat with palm trees and the ocean. I desperately wanted serenity and a healing program to engage in. As I looked over what the retreats offered, including serene meditation spots, yoga, sound healing, beautiful gardens, surfing, healing groups, and rooms filled with flowers and open windows, I could feel how this environment would help my body progress in healing. After narrowing down the many choices, I really wanted to go to a Bali Goddess Retreat or to Costa Rica for surfing and yoga. It would be wonderful to spend ten days in the healing offered through landscape, meditation, yoga, support groups, and professional instruction.

I never made it to Bali or Costa Rica. There are times I regret not finding a way to go, but responsibilities and financial restraints pulled me away from what the broken parts of my body desperately needed. The challenge in the aftermath of the *Storm Phase* and during the *Clearing Phase* is rebalancing life's demands. Constraints of employment, caretaking, relationships, finances, and countless other responsibilities do not lessen after trauma. In many cases they increase. Each of us will have to work with the tools and resources we can access. Some may have the time and resources to fly across the world for a 10-day, all-inclusive healing retreat. Others might create their own sanctuary with weekend hikes in the mountains or a night away in a hotel while attending a local support group. Whatever your resources allow, make time to rest and retreat in whatever way possible, even if it's an hour soaking in a bath reading or listening to your favorite music.

Everyone's journey will be different based on their resources and what speaks to them. Our goal is to do the best we can with what we have and continue to put one foot in front of the other. For me, the specific retreats to a tropical destination did not play out. I talked myself out of taking time off work and spending money because it felt too stressful. At times I find myself wanting to go. I envision the floral aroma of the healing gardens, lying on a bed surrounded by tropical flowers with the ocean breeze blowing through the windows. Perhaps in the future that will take place. Do I think it could have helped further my healing? Yes, I think it would have. But I know I am doing my best with what I have, and I trust you are doing the same.

Activities

1. Research potential local or international retreats that your body connects with and would bring you peace and joy.
2. If you can book a retreat, then do it! If not, create a folder of ideas or vision board of a future retreat that you will work towards.
3. Find local retreats – such as a community drum circle, a walking group, a renaissance fair, a sing along. Any activity that uplifts and empowers you.

Sources

1 Ward, K. P., Wood, D. S., & Young, T. M. (2020). Retreat Intervention Effectiveness for Female Survivors of Child Sexual Abuse. Research on Social Work Practice.

CHAPTER 29

SLEEP & EXERCISE

Foundations of Health and Healing

If you think you can't, change your mind.

— Denis Morton

An often-dismissed but key aspect of trauma recovery is the incorporation of healthy sleep patterns and regular exercise. There is a reason healthcare professionals consistently remind us to exercise and get plenty of sleep. Sleep and exercise are as essential as food and water for the body and mind to be in its healthiest state.

Sleep

After a traumatic event, anxiety and depressive symptoms usually have an impact on sleep patterns. They may cause insomnia, sleeping too much, restless sleep, or nightmares.

Despite my childhood trauma, which often causes sleep disturbances, I was blessed to be a sound sleeper and rarely had issues. I have always loved sleeping. In fact, this came to light when my son's kindergarten teacher was helping him fill out my Mother's Day card and asked him, "What does your mom like to do?" He responded, "My mom loves to sleep, rest, and lay down." Don't you love a child's honest perception? With an answer like that, it is hard to imagine that I was ever productive, let alone raised four children. But he definitely understood I was a fan of sleeping!

It was difficult to relate to others who had difficulty with their sleep patterns because I hadn't experienced what that was like—until

I did! The impact of my traumatic experience caused sleepless nights, nightmares, and difficulty waking up. My sleep was not regulated, so I began taking melatonin supplements and over-the-counter medication to help me rest. Thankfully, as I have progressed in my healing journey, my body is settling down more, and I am able to sleep the recommended 7-9 hours a night. There are still nights when I have trauma nightmares. They are usually triggered by a circumstance associated with my trauma or something I watched in a movie or TV show that felt familiar to my experience. When I have a nightmare or sleep disturbance, I know it is a sign that my body is not feeling healthy and safe. This reminds me to place a higher priority on incorporating a healing activity into my schedule the next day to help my body feel balanced and in control. This might be going to yoga, going for a bike ride, or rocking out to some dance songs.

Most of my clients experience unhealthy sleep patterns after a trauma *Storm*. While it is challenging, it is a normal process after trauma. Some clients are afraid to go to sleep. Some are afraid to wake up and face reality, and still others may experience a combination of both. Creating new sleep patterns can be one of the more complicated parts of recovery, but it is worth the effort. Healthy sleep patterns decrease stress, regulate the immune system, and lower anxiety.[1] Sleep also keeps the brain strong, affecting memory, decision-making, problem-solving, creativity, and how we process emotions.[2]

As you begin to implement healthy sleep patterns, here are some helpful suggestions from the Sleep Foundation:

- **Maintain a regular sleep schedule:** Try your best to go to sleep and get up at the same time every day. This helps train your body to rest at certain times.
- **Sleep where you feel safe:** After a traumatic event, you may have a hard time calming down enough to fall asleep. Take some time to think about what changes you could make to create a calm, safe sleeping space. You might consider keeping

a nightlight on, having a trusted loved one sleep close by, or keeping your phone close.

- **Engage in relaxing activities:** Try some relaxation exercises to calm your body and prepare it for sleep. Reading, listening to calming music, or mindfulness activities are some examples.
- **Do not force sleep:** If sleep just isn't coming, it may be more beneficial to get up and do something else for a while. Make sure it is a calm, quiet activity. Once you start to feel tired again, go back to bed.
- **Seek professional care:** There are many people ready and able to help you process your trauma so you can regain your mental and physical health.[3]

Exercise

During the *Storm* and *Clearing Phase,* it was a daily fight to keep my anxiety down. I had to work to avoid buying into the negative messaging spewed from the trauma. If I didn't, the anxiety could plunge me down a rabbit hole of self-doubt. Exercising became key to regulating my trauma responses. Whenever I engage in physical activity, I feel an immediate and noticeable difference in my body and mind. It reduces my anxiety, and I feel more empowered and confident. I have always loved being physically active, so exercising may come easier to me than it might to others. In working with clients, some individuals are naturally drawn to exercise and sporting activities. Others, however, find exercising more difficult and require greater effort. Not everyone has the same physical response to exercise. The important thing is to find a type of exercise that fits your unique needs. It may be walking, running, biking, hiking, skiing, water aerobics, strength training or joining community classes —really anything that you can muster up the courage to do regularly.

There were many days I would grab my running shoes and run up the mountain or hook my bike up on the back of my Jeep and head to a beautiful trail. As I pushed myself, I could feel my mood stabilize, my thoughts became clearer, and I felt empowered. This happens because exercise changes chemical levels in the brain. Stress hormones decrease, while serotonin and endorphins increase. After exercising, you may find that you can focus better, feel more alert, and have a more positive outlook.

No matter the level of motivation or desire for exercise, research has shown many times over that regular exercise is effective in improving mental health, overcoming depression, and other challenges. Exercise can be as effective as antidepressant medication, without the possible negative side effects. A Harvard study even showed that 15 minutes of running or an hour of walking each day reduces the risk of developing major depression by 26%.[4]

How much do I need to exercise?

The *U.S. Department of Health and Human Services* recommends getting at least 150 minutes of moderate aerobic activity, 75 minutes of vigorous exercise, or a combination of the two each week. If these numbers seem daunting, remember that any amount of exercise is better than none.[5]

Be creative when you think about ways to exercise and be physically active. You may take a dance class, join a walking group, sign up for a Zumba class, find friends to play pickleball with, play tag with your grandchildren, or walk the dog a little longer. At work you might consider adding a pedal cycler under your desk, taking the stairs instead of the elevator, or parking your car further from the entrance so you have more time to get in your steps. There are countless YouTube fitness videos available and thrift stores offer old exercise videos on DVD. Explore the best ways to incorporate physical activity that feels enjoyable and attainable into your daily life. Your body and mind will love the effort.

Activities

1. Try a new sport or exercise class.
2. Assess your nightly routine to see if you can incorporate calming activities, or if need to, adjust your bedding for more comfort.
3. Investigate sleep apps with nature sounds, white noise or green noise.

Sources

1 *Stress - How sleep can affect stress levels | Banner Health.* (n.d.). https://www.bannerhealth.com/healthcareblog/teach-me/how-sleep-can-affect-stress

2 Suni, E., & Suni, E. (2023, July 18). *How lack of sleep impacts cognitive performance and focus.* Sleep Foundation. https://www.sleepfoundation.org/sleep-deprivation/lack-of-sleep-and-cognitive-impairment

3 Sleep Foundation. (2023, November 16). *Trauma and sleep.* https://www.sleepfoundation.org/mental-health/trauma-and-sleep

4 Department of Health & Human Services. (n.d.). *Exercise and mental health.* Better Health Channel. https://www.betterhealth.vic.gov.au/health/healthyliving/exercise-and-mental-health

5 *Depression and anxiety: Exercise eases symptoms.* (n.d.). Mayo Clinic. https://www.mayoclinic.org/diseases-conditions/depression/in-depth/depression-and-exercise/art-20046495

CHAPTER 30

SUNLIGHT & COLOR

Light Up My World

It is during our darkest moments that we must focus to see the light.

— Aristotle Onassis

During a trauma *Storm*, it takes intentional effort to look for light. It can seem as if darkness wants to consume us. During the *Clearing Phase*, we can see glimpses of the contrast between light and darkness through a magnified lens. There is a need for beautiful light and colors to remind us of hope, beauty, and joy—of life before trauma. When deciding on a name for my counseling company, I wanted to symbolize the idea of light. I chose the name Lucent Counseling & Consulting, which means, "glowing with light and marked by clarity."[1] The message of light and hope was something I wanted to portray in the name—a lighthouse beacon guiding a ship in distress to safety.

Looking for light is critical during trauma recovery. Archbishop Desmond Tutu said it best, "Hope is being able to see there is light, despite all the darkness."[2]

Sunlight

Sunlight serves as a powerful healing tool. As research on sunshine's beneficial effects on mental health grows, it is increasingly recognized as essential to healing. In my work as a trauma therapist, I've witnessed clients thrive with sunshine, feeling more rejuvenated and empowered when they access those healing rays. Early morning or evening sunlight has the greatest effect, while any sunshine supports mood regulation, vitamin D absorption and many other bodily processes. Sunlight cues certain areas in the retina, which trigger the release of serotonin.[3] Amongst other benefits, serotonin aids our body in regulating our mood and balancing sleep. Neuroscientist Andrew Huberman, discusses the benefits of morning sunlight in his podcast, *Huberman Lab*, sharing that "consistently getting morning light can significantly impact overall wellness." Exposure to morning sunlight helps set your internal clock, aligning your sleep-wake cycle with the natural day-night cycle. This alignment is essential for maintaining consistent sleep patterns and overall well-being.[4]

Knowing the benefits of sunshine, I used sun exposure as a main tool in my trauma healing. Spending time outside relieved that constant physical anxiety and set me at ease. In fact, there were times I would just lie on the grass or snow and let the sunrays comfort and absorb into my body. Whether I was sitting, walking, hiking, or biking, the sun rejuvenated my body and lifted my spirits. For me, there was something much deeper too, like a connection to the heavens providing comfort and healing. In my physical spaces, I purposely opened up all the curtains or blinds, put my home desk by a window, and positioned my chair in my counseling office to face the window. I was intentionally trying to absorb sunlight to increase my serotonin and vitamin D absorption.

Many studies reveal the benefits of sunlight on mental health. One study reported by UCLA Health concluded that "each additional hour spent outside in natural light was linked to a corresponding decrease in the risk of developing long-term depression. They also saw reduced use of antidepressants, as well as self-reported improvements to mood and general feelings of happiness."[5] Another study found that even 20 minutes outside in nice weather provided benefits such as increased mood, improved memory, and more creative thinking.[6] These are benefits I want to experience, even though I am now past my trauma *Storm* and enjoying life.

Sun Lamps

There are times when being in natural light is difficult. Working in an environment with limited natural light, working long hours during the winter when it is dark when you come and go, responsibilities with children, medical limitations, and more can inhibit your ability to be outside. In these cases, you may find benefits in using artificial sun lamps. Sun lamps can have the same serotonin-producing effect as the sun; however, they do not stimulate vitamin D production like the sun. Ideally, a sun lamp should be used for at least 20 minutes in the morning and must be used daily to gain maximum benefit. Note that it may take a week or two to notice the benefits.[7]

As you implement natural sun or sun lamps into your healing tool kit, it is advised to work with your medical provider to understand exposure risks.

Colors

An activity I find beneficial when working with clients is finding how each person visualizes emotions in color. Interestingly, the knowledge of how color can impact the body, and mind goes back thousands of years. The Egyptians believed certain colors had healing properties. Orange, for example, was thought to reduce fatigue, so they painted therapy rooms orange. Blue was believed to relieve pain, and purple was used to improve skin conditions. Color therapy was also common in *Ayurveda*, an ancient system of medicine developed in India, and in traditional Chinese medicine. Modern studies have confirmed that color may not be able to heal certain health problems, but color can lower blood pressure, influence mood, affect appetite, boost creativity, and more.[8]

When I visualized my trauma, the colors were black and gray, whereas peace and love were baby blue, and happiness and joy felt like yellow and pink. Colors of emotions will be different for each person. The color experiment encourages you to visualize colors throughout your day. As I was actively going through my *Storm* and *Clearing Phase*, I found myself in a lot of black and gray moments, but I would purposely create moments that would bring in baby blue, yellow, or pink emotions, even if only for short moments. It is an intentional effort that teaches your brain to allow color to influence your thoughts and mood, focusing on bringing in happier colors.

Through your healing journey, I would encourage you to think about the colors you are surrounding yourself with in your home or office space. Do the colors match the mood and emotions you want your body to experience? Even if you aren't able to make many changes in these spaces, such as painting a wall, you could add a splash of color through art or fabrics. Since I wanted to experience more joy in my life, I added the colors I associated with joy into my home and office, and I encourage you to find more sunlight and color every day of your life.

Activities

1. Schedule more time out in the sun. Open a window. Go for a walk during lunch break at work. Move your chair closer to the window.
2. If you have Seasonal Affective Disorder (winter depression), invest in a sun lamp and commit to sit by it daily.
3. Add more colors into your space that helps you feel peace and joy.

Sources

1 Merriam-Webster. (n.d.). Lucent. In Merriam-Webster.com dictionary. Retrieved January 27, 2025, from https://www.merriam-webster.com/dictionary/lucent

2 Desmond Tutu Quotes. (n.d.). BrainyQuote.com. Retrieved January 27, 2025, from BrainyQuote.com Web site: https://www.brainyquote.com/quotes/desmond_tutu_45412

3 Crna, R. N. M. (2019, April 1). *What are the benefits of sunlight?* Healthline. https://www.healthline.com/health/depression/benefits-sunlight

4 Hattar, Samer and Huberman, Andrew. HubermanLab.com. Retrieved January 27, 2025, from https://ai.hubermanlab.com/c/a22fb27e-cab9-11ef-b665-83117706f7aa

5 *Being in natural light improves mood, increases happiness.* (n.d.). UCLA Health. https://www.uclahealth.org/news/article/being-in-natural-light-improves-mood-increases-happiness

6 Achor, S. (2011b). *The happiness advantage: The Seven Principles of Positive Psychology that Fuel Success and Performance at Work, 53.* Random House.

7 Haase, M. (2024, November 9). This natural treatment may help with depression, study finds. *Prevention.* https://www.prevention.com/health/mental-health/a62854676/bright-light-therapy-for-depression-study

8 Nicola, S. (2024, June 24). *What is color psychology?* WebMD. https://www.webmd.com/mental-health/what-is-color-psychology

CHAPTER 31

SUPPORT ANIMALS

You're My Best Friend

Animals are such agreeable friends—they ask no questions; they pass no criticisms.

— George Elliott

As a practitioner, I have not worked with or trained support animals, but there is solid research that demonstrates animals or pets can be a contributing source of social support and stress reduction in trauma recovery.[1] As a teen, I found comfort and calm cuddling with our family's black lab, Raspberry, and my sister's horse, Cinnamon. My horse, Honey, was not the nurturing kind—not all animals provide the same type of emotional support! When I was feeling down or needing connection, Raspberry and Cinnamon would provide the nurturing and connection I needed to help me reset. Both Raspberry and Cinnamon seemed to embrace the role and appeared to find satisfaction with the connection. When I spent time with them, my mood improved, I felt loved, and my body relaxed.

My children found this same comfort with our family golden retriever, Cheerio, when they were growing up. Cheerio was a natural nurturer and reminded me of the caregiving dog Nana in the Peter Pan story. I could see that when my kids needed some extra love and comfort, Cheerio was able to fill that need. One of my sons captured his relationship with Cheerio in a self-portrait he drew in high school. His artwork hangs in my home office. If you look closely, you will see the sketch is composed of words that reflected his thoughts about his relationship with Cheerio, including such phrases as, "Comfort. I love you.

I had a bad day. It's okay. You're my best friend." I believe this drawing not only encapsulates my son's relationship with Cheerio but also how many people feel about their emotional support animals.

When working with clients who choose to get an emotional support animal, the changes are striking. Animals provide comfort, nurturing, love, and healing, and I have witnessed emotional and mind-body transformation after a client accepted an animal into their home. Caring for a pet that offers unconditional love helps us heal from trauma. Pets help us get out of bed when we don't always want to. They connect us to the environment and give us a purpose.[2]

One friend, exhausted in mind, body and spirit from spending her days in the ICU with a dying family member found unexpected solace in feeding a stray cat near her home. The cat had been left behind on the property of an old friend who had since passed, now abandoned as the land was being repurposed. Though she knew she couldn't catch the skinny, little, raggedy, feral cat, she could feed it—allowing her to keep it alive. It was a strange but powerful solace, comforting her when she felt powerless to do the same for her loved one. In nurturing the cat, she found purpose. Though she was helpless to stop the suffering and death of her loved one, she could relieve some suffering for a little cat. Years later, the details of her loved one's raw and painful death have faded, but she remembers the tranquility of feeding that little feral cat.

Benefits of Animal Support

According to *Johns Hopkins Medicine*, simply petting a dog can lower levels of cortisol, the hormone linked to stress, while interactions with dogs elevate oxytocin, the bonding hormone found in mother-infant connections. A recent survey showed that 84% of PTSD sufferers with service dogs experienced major symptom relief, with 40% decreasing their medication use.[3]

Emotional Support Animal vs. Service Dogs

The Animal Kennel Club provides information on the differences between emotional support animals (ESAs) and task-trained service dogs:

> *Emotional Support Animals (ESAs) provide support through companionship and can help ease anxiety, depression, and certain phobias. However, they are not service dogs, and ESA users do not receive the same accommodations as service dog users. A service dog, such as a guide dog or psychiatric service dog, is generally allowed anywhere the public is allowed; ESAs are not. For example, ESAs generally cannot accompany their owners into restaurants or shopping malls... Individuals who use ESAs are provided certain accommodations under federal law in the areas of housing and air travel. The Fair Housing Act includes ESAs in its definition of assistance animals. Under the act, people cannot be discriminated against due to disability when obtaining housing. Rules such as pet bans or restrictions are waived for people who have a prescription for an ESA, and they cannot be charged a pet deposit for having their ESA live with them.*[4]

Obtaining an ESA Letter

Some situations require an Emotional Support Animal letter. ESA letters can be written by licensed professionals such as primary care physicians, psychologists, or licensed therapists. As professionals, they can determine if a patient or client needs an ESA for their psychological and emotional well-being.[5] It is important to remember that laws regarding ESAs and service dogs are in constant motion and depend on each state and country's legislation, so if you own an ESA or service dog, stay updated on current laws in your area.

What to Consider

Caring for an animal is a long-term commitment that must be considered carefully. Animals require time and money, which can add stress and must be taken into account when making the decision to bring an animal into the home. Consult your individual state laws and regulations to understand your local laws concerning Emotional Support Animals in public places.

Some questions to consider:

- *Do I have the time and energy to properly train an animal?*
- *Do I have time for the animal's daily care?*
- *Do I have the patience to care for an animal?*
- *Will the animal contribute any additional life stressors?*
- *Can I take on the expenses associated with food, toys, veterinary bills, and grooming?*
- *How will an animal impact my social interactions and lifestyle?*
- *Is my home set up to safely accommodate a pet?*

Even if you are unable to have an animal in your home to provide emotional support, finding time to interact with animals can be healing. Local animal rescue or shelter has openings for volunteers to walk, clean, or spend time with animals. While in the *Clearing Phase* of my recovery, I took riding lessons to connect with horses, as horses are the animal that brings me the most connection and uplifts my spirits. I don't own a horse, but I can be intentional about finding time to spend with horses. You don't have to have a pet, ESA, or service dog to benefit from the healing properties of animals. The focus is to be intentional about implementing tools that can help us transform trauma into hope and healing.

Activities

1. Visit a petting zoo, stop by a pet store you can interact with the animals, or volunteer at a local animal shelter.
2. Look for equine therapy lessons in your community, go on a horseback riding trail ride, participate in yoga classes that have animals, or visit a local barn.
3. Assess if a therapy animal is right for you, and if so, what type of animal? A cat, dog, turtle, snake, gerbil, cow, horse?

Sources

1 Dominick, W., Walenski-Geml, A., & Taku, K. (2020). Associations Between Pet Ownership, Posttraumatic Growth, and Stress Symptoms in Adolescents. *Anthrozoös, 33*(4), 547–560. https://doi.org/10.1080/08927936.2020.1771059

2 Sutton, J., PhD. (2021). *Pets & Wellbeing: 15 Benefits of Emotional Support Animals.* Positivepsychology.com. https://positivepsychology.com/pets-mental-health/

3 John Hopkins Medicine. (n.d.). *The Friend Who Keeps You Young.* hopkinsmedicine.org. Retrieved January 11, 2025, from https://www.hopkinsmedicine.org/health/wellness-and-prevention/the-friend-who-keeps-you-young

4 Gibeault, S. (2021, February 24). *Everything you need to know about emotional support animals.* American Kennel Club. https://www.akc.org/expert-advice/news/everything-about-emotional-support-animals/

5 Fleming, M. (n.d.). *Who can write an ESA letter? (Full list + online options).* Pettable. https://pettable.com/blog/who-can-write-an-esa-letter

CHAPTER 32

THERAPISTS

Finding the Right One for You

You are the one thing in this world, above all other things, that you must never give up on.

— Lili Reinhart

I have found much joy and satisfaction in observing clients work through their trauma and feel more in control of their lives and relationships. Therapists have the privilege of witnessing some of the most wonderful transformations, whether a client is freed from the weight of emotional chains they have carried for decades due to rape or abuse, gains skills to improve their relationships, or make needed changes in existing toxic relationship or behaviors. I witnessed clients grow in many ways, such as by setting and meeting goals of running in half marathons or being able to engage in life after a significant death. Human trafficking survivors have become advocates for other survivors and people have found a path forward after divorce, tackled overwhelming anxiety, and broken free after years of debilitating depression. Therapy works. Individuals have proven through history that they are resilient, and with the right interventions, hope and healing are possible. Therapy can be challenging and takes time, money, and intentional work, but the effort can lead to a more joyful, productive, and peaceful life.

Many wonder, "How do I find a good therapist?" As with any profession, you might need to explore until you find the right therapist for you. If you were trying to find a medical specialist you trust with the right knowledge and skills for your condition, you would search around, and this is true when finding a mental health therapist too. Therapy, no matter how old or young we are, allows us to evaluate how the past is impacting our current behaviors and thoughts. It aids in assessing the health of our relationships and helps screen whether we are living as the best and healthiest version of ourselves, on a path focused on peace and joy. Therapy can be very insightful and life-changing!

Individuals experiencing trauma-related depression, anxiety, or PTSD symptoms should seek therapy from a therapist trained in trauma. For my trauma healing journey, I looked for a female therapist who was trained in trauma interventions. Her gentle personality set me at ease. I felt like I was talking to a friend. She was also familiar with my faith, which was important for me during the healing process. As you look for a therapist, find one who aligns with your needs, understands your background, and is someone with whom you can communicate well. My therapist has been the right fit for me and has been a great resource and support during my healing process. Early on in your sessions, if you feel it's not a good fit, find someone you can relate well with. A study by Safran and Muran found that a trusting partnership between you and your therapist is one of the strongest predictors of effective therapy.[1] In my practice, I encourage my clients that if they do not feel that comfort and connection with me within the first three to four sessions, to continue to search for the right therapist for their situation because my goal is for them to succeed.

One woman shared her frustration with seeing a therapist who always wore a very wrinkled shirt. As a perfectionist, those wrinkles made it difficult for her to concentrate on therapy. The details matter, so listen to your needs. When looking for a therapist, there are things to consider regarding comfort and connection. For instance, would you feel more comfortable with a particular gender, age, religion, race, sexuality, or special certification? Is there a particular physical appearance that feels more comfortable to you? How does the office space feel? You may also consider your therapist's attire, whether casual or business wear, and how it makes you feel. My advice is to listen to what your body and mind are telling you. As you start your search, I would recommend asking friends, family, and people in your community circle if anyone has recommendations and why they liked that particular therapist.

There are also online resources that give therapist bios, pictures, and contact information. A commonly used site to locate therapists is *psychologytoday.com*. On the site, you can put in your area code and insurance, along with your individual preferences, and the site will generate a list of therapists who match the provided criteria. Your insurance company also might be able to provide bios for therapists on their provider list. The *Mental Health America* website has specific information on types of mental health clinicians and can connect you with help in your area.[2]

Considerations When Looking for a Therapist

Traditional In-Person Therapy

Sessions are generally booked for one hour. As with other professional fees, the hourly charge for a therapist might feel hefty, and therapy can potentially last for months or sometimes years, depending on the therapeutic need and goals. Most insurance companies cover mental health therapy either by setting a co-pay rate specific to mental health therapy or putting the fee towards the deductible until the deductible is met. Therapists also offer private pay. If paying the hourly fee is a hindrance, I recommend looking for a therapy practice with a master-level intern, as they charge a lower hourly rate. You could also search for a community-based non-profit or ecclesiastical therapy program with a sliding fee scale or financial assistance.

Intensive Session Options

Some therapists, like myself, also offer private-pay intensive trauma therapy sessions which can last 2-6 hours in a day for more rapid results and can be booked for multiple days in a row. These are usually cash pay as insurance doesn't cover extended sessions.

Consultation

When looking for a therapist, some therapists offer a free consultation so clients can ask questions, allowing the client and therapist to assess whether it is the right therapeutic fit.

Modality: In-person, Telehealth, or Hybrid?

There are multiple formats available for therapy sessions. There are in-person sessions where you and your therapist are together in the office, telehealth sessions provided through a HIPAA-compliant online program, or hybrid models that can switch between in-person and telehealth depending on the availability of the client and therapist. In-person or telehealth sessions, or a combination of both, are effective, and insurance will generally pay for either type of session.[3]

Therapist vs. Life Coach

As life coaching has become more common, questions have arisen about the difference between a therapist and a life coach. The primary difference is that therapists must be in good standing, must have passed rigorous credentialing, must have formal schooling with additional training hours, and are regulated by the state licensing board.[4] This includes thousands of hours of clinical practice under the supervision of a licensed practitioner before becoming fully licensed. Mental health therapists are also able to diagnose mental health conditions and can engage in interventions to go deep into past work and trauma. Life coaches are not obligated to hold formal qualifications, testing, or experience with proven methods.

Both mental health therapy and life coaching have value but in different areas. Both professions can work on current and future goals. Insurance companies do not pay for life coaching, but life coaches can also meet in your home, out for a walk, or in a community space. Note that clients can have mental health therapists and life coaches at the same time to meet different goals. For the most effective impact, inform both professionals of the other treatments and goals being worked on.

Trauma Informed vs. Trauma Trained Therapist

When looking for a trauma therapist, I would recommend a therapist who is *trauma trained,* meaning the therapist has engaged in higher-level training and certification specific to evidence-based trauma interventions. Therapists who are *trauma-informed* may have general knowledge of how trauma impacts a client, but they don't have specific training or certifications.

Multiple Therapists

There are times when a client might find it beneficial to work with multiple therapists who are trained in different modalities. For instance, a client might be seeing a couple's therapist with their partner while having individual trauma therapy sessions. Or a client might be working with a therapist for a specific mental health intervention, while also working on a specific trauma with a trauma trained therapist. When working with multiple therapists, it is helpful to inform each professional of the therapeutic goals being worked on with the other therapist, and you may need to sign a release for the therapists to work together on your desired treatment goals. When the client feels the resources and interventions of a particular therapist have been completed, the client can seek out another therapist with additional resources and interventions to complete the therapeutic goals and healing.

Efficacy of Therapy

Therapy can feel daunting. It requires time and dedication, and there is usually a cost. But it is effective! Some clients are in therapy for a short period of time and find solutions. Others have more complicated challenges and may need long-term therapy, meaning months or years to work through complex issues. Psychotherapy improves the emotional well-being of clients, which surprisingly leads to increased work satisfaction, fewer sick days, better health, and less disability.[5] With the right therapist, therapy works!

Activities

1. Ask friends, family and colleagues if they have recommendations for therapists.
2. Write a list of qualities that you would prefer the therapist to have that would make you feel more at ease and connected.
3. Research online potential therapists and reach out to set up an appointment.

Sources

1 Goldsmith, J. (2013). The value of difficult moments in the Client-Therapist relationship. *Clinical Science Insights.* https://www.family-institute.org/sites/default/files/pdfs/csi_goldsmith_therapist_relationship.pdf

2 *Types of mental health professionals.* (n.d.). Mental Health America. https://mhanational.org/types-mental-health-professionals

3 Ko, N. J. (2024, April 10). Virtual Therapy vs. In-Person therapy | Psychology.org. *Psychology.org | Psychology's Comprehensive Online Resource.* https://www.psychology.org/resources/virtual-therapy-vs-in-person

4 Hemendinger, E. (2024, September 10). Life coach or therapist? Know the differences. *NPR.* https://www.npr.org/sections/shots-health-news/2024/09/09/nx-s1-5106771/coach-coaching-therapy-differences-mental-health

5 *What is Psychotherapy?* (2025). American Psychiatry Association (APA). Retrieved January 21, 2025, from https://www.psychiatry.org/patients-families/psychotherapy

CHAPTER 33

TRAUMA THERAPEUTIC MODALITIES

Current Treatment Options

Taking care of your mental health is an act of self-love.

— Anonymous

When finding a trauma therapist to work with, it is important to be familiar with evidence-based trauma modalities that are effective in reducing anxiety, depression, and PTSD symptoms. There is no one-size-fits-all method, and the healing journey might require patience while exploring multiple interventions to see what works best for you. Some methods might be very effective for one individual but less effective for another. Individual therapists will have specific modalities they are trained in and feel comfortable implementing when working with clients—no two therapists are alike. For instance, I am an EMDR-trained therapist, but I also like to add interventions from Cognitive Behavioral Therapy (CBT), Solution-Focused Therapy, Strengths-Based Therapy, and Talk Therapy. As a therapist, I have connected with these modalities, but other therapists will have a different collection of modalities they feel comfortable with and implement.

During my healing journey, the modalities I chose to work with for myself were EMDR, Talk Therapy, and Neurofeedback. Below is a quick reference guide to the interventions commonly used during trauma work. I encourage you to further research the modalities you would like to implement in your recovery.

Accelerated Resolution Therapy (ART)

Accelerated Resolution Therapy is what it sounds like—an evidence-based psychotherapy intended to work quickly to relieve trauma, anxiety, and depression symptoms. It often uses guided imagery and other relaxation techniques, which help people work through and process their trauma without having to talk through all the details. An important feature of ART is using eye movements to help the brain reorganize memories and emotions and restore positive thoughts in place of negative ones. This can help relieve nightmares, panic attacks, and phobias stemming from trauma.[1]

> ***My Thoughts:***
> *I am not trained in ART, but I have fellow clinicians who are ART-certified. These colleagues have reported that they find the ART modality to be effective. ART has a similar pattern to EMDR but also has some differences.*

Art Therapy

Art therapists are credential-holding professionals who combine art making and creativity with their knowledge of clinical skills and psychological theory. Some people may find it easier to express themselves in art rather than language, so art therapy would be a good option for them.[2]

> ***My Thoughts:***
> *I have never participated in art therapy, but I have a friend who is trained in art therapy and works effectively with clients who have experienced trauma; she reports positive results.*

Cognitive Behavioral Therapy (CBT)

The purpose of Cognitive Behavioral Therapy is to help you recognize thought patterns and behaviors that are hindering your progress and healing. You will explore how your emotions affect your behavior and learn ways to change your behavior for good. It focuses on what you are doing now instead of what has happened in the past. The point is to learn positive coping strategies so you can move forward toward a happy and productive future. It might include learning how to face fears and challenging situations, perhaps through role play or homework; learning to judge the accuracy of your thoughts and how they might be holding you back; and gaining confidence in yourself and your ability to handle challenges.[3]

My Thoughts:
Cognitive Behavioral Therapy is one of the most common modalities used in therapy and is usually implemented alongside other modalities. It is effective for learning new thought patterns and behaviors. I implement this modality with my clients and have seen positive results.

Cognitive Processing Therapy (CPT)

Cognitive Processing Therapy is more intense, consisting of about 12 sessions, 60-90 minutes each, depending on client needs. It involves learning about how trauma affects our thought patterns and learning new strategies to identify, challenge, and change inaccurate and unhelpful thoughts.[4] You may be asked to write about your traumatic experience and the impact it had on you. It may include homework to practice the things you are learning.[5]

My Thoughts:
I am not familiar with CPT, but the research does show that it is an effective treatment for PTSD.

Eye Movement Desensitization and Reprocessing (EMDR)

Eye Movement Desensitization and Reprocessing therapy is a mental health treatment that involves moving your eyes in a certain way as you process traumatic memories and emotions. It doesn't require recounting details of traumatic events but instead focuses on the emotions and thoughts connected to them. This helps you heal and move forward.[6]

My Thoughts:
I am an EMDR-trained therapist and am an advocate for EMDR therapy because I have witnessed positive results not only in myself, but also with clients. EMDR reduces symptoms and negative beliefs that are associated with specific trauma events. I love being an EMDR therapist and seeing my clients feel more in control of their trauma symptoms.

Exposure Therapy

Exposure therapy helps people overcome the fears that are holding them back from fully experiencing life. These fears can be specific objects, activities, or situations. In Exposure therapy, clients confront their fears in a safe and controlled way, helping to break patterns of avoidance and fear.[7] Exposure therapy has variations of types of exposure depending on the client's needs. Exposure therapy is an effective modality in overcoming phobias and specific fears, including those related to trauma experiences.

My Thoughts:
I have worked with clients on challenging themselves on specific fears that they desired to overcome, such as attending a concert, talking to someone in class, driving a car, etc. by creating small goals of exposure. The client keeps increasing goals of exposure until they meet their ultimate goal.

Ketamine

Ketamine is an option for people with depression who are unable to get relief from other treatments. Studies have shown promising results regarding the drug's impact on various mental health conditions, including anxiety, severe depression and PTSD. Used in low doses, ketamine alters levels of glutamate, a chemical messenger in the brain, which can result in new neural connections. The brain becomes more adaptable and creates new pathways, giving patients the opportunity to develop more positive thoughts and feelings.[8] Ketamine is administered at therapeutic ketamine clinics by medical professionals through

IV fluids or injections, or can be prescribed by psychiatrists. Patients will receive the necessary doses over weeks or months. It is recommended to seek psychotherapy while receiving ketamine treatments. Ketamine currently is not covered by most insurance plans and can cost thousands of dollars.

> ***My Thoughts:***
> *I became familiar with ketamine clinics around 2018 when new clinics were opening in my state. I was skeptical at first, but after seeing positive results with my clients who have received treatments, I feel that it is a resource worth considering for people with chronic depression and PTSD. The cost can be significant, but individuals who have suffered from chronic depression for years have felt it was worth the investment.*

Massage Therapy

(Note: this intervention is not provided by a mental health professional)
Most people are probably familiar with massages. It has been shown to provide relief, not just from physical strain, but also with emotional and mental tension. These benefits, though anecdotal, clients have shared improvements in depression, anxiety, and other unwelcome symptoms that may stem from trauma. Massage therapy may also help you feel more comfortable and safer in your own body.[9]

> ***My Thoughts:***
> *During my trauma and healing process, I found my muscles to be extremely tight and painful at times, particularly in my neck and jaw. Sometimes I would get a deep massage to really work out the tension, but other times I needed more of a mild, calming massage to help my body relax and self-regulate. For me, I felt it was a beneficial intervention, especially with physical aches and pain. Massage therapy is not covered by most insurance companies, so it is often self-pay.*

Medical Marijuana (Cannabis)

"There are currently no psychiatric indications approved by the U.S. Food and Drug Administration (FDA) for cannabinoids, and there is limited evidence supporting the therapeutic use of cannabinoids for treatment of psychiatric disorders."[10]

> ***My Thoughts:***
> *Over the past several years, there has been growing discussion in the medical community regarding the effectiveness of medical marijuana in treating trauma/PTSD symptoms. While there are reported benefits, there are also risks that include increased anxiety, psychological dependence, and other medical complications.*[11] *I know the discussion has come up frequently in my own practice as medical marijuana has been legalized where I practice. I have seen it work really well for some clients, but not for others. Clinical studies show mixed results. Further research is needed. My recommendation would be to meet with a medical doctor who prescribes medical marijuana to discuss the pros and cons of consumption, along with your mental health provider. It is important to study the laws in your own state regarding the use of medical marijuana.*

MDMA

MDMA is a stimulant drug that increases the release of dopamine and serotonin in the brain but also has many serious adverse effects. There is much discussion in the therapy and legislative world regarding the potential of using MDMA to manage trauma symptoms. The FDA has not yet approved MDMA for use. However, both the medical community and lawmakers across the country are actively studying its effectiveness and determining how to treat patients responsibly. In the state where I live, the legislature recently approved a pilot program to study and implement MDMA use with patients.

My Thoughts:
There appears to be promising research that MDMA has healing benefits for mental health, and I have heard testimonials of individuals who have accessed it in other countries and found it beneficial for trauma recovery. As it is not approved by the FDA at this time, if this were an intervention you would like to explore, I encourage you to continue to research, follow your state legislation, and discuss the options with your medical and mental health providers.

Narrative Therapy

The goal of narrative therapy is to separate an individual from their problems so they can view them from an outside lens. This prevents them from internalizing problems and makes it easier to find solutions. It may include deconstructing a traumatic experience, storytelling, and changing the narrative they tell themselves. It relies on each person's individual values and skills to help them navigate challenges.[12]

My Thoughts:
I am not trained in narrative therapy, but it is an accepted and evidence-based trauma modality.

Psychotherapy/Talk Therapy

Talk therapy, also known as psychotherapy is a common therapeutic approach. It's how counseling is most frequently portrayed in television shows and movies. It is a structured dialogue with a therapist, working through issues, identifying problems and setting goals.[13]

My Thoughts:
Talk therapy is the basic modality used in counseling and can be implemented with other modalities. It is effective in processing thoughts and feelings and aids the body in processing emotions and thoughts. For trauma work, I recommend implementing talk therapy along with other evidence-based modalities.

Neurofeedback Therapy (EEG Biofeedback)

Neurofeedback is an intervention that uses computer-based programs to monitor brainwave activity. Patients are given visual or auditory signals. On a screen, the patient's brainwaves are shown, allowing them to see how their brainwave patterns respond to the signals in real-time. This helps patients modify their thought patterns as needed and learn to regulate their own brain function and improve in desired areas.[14] The studies regarding neurofeedback are inconclusive, and treatments can cost thousands of dollars and may require multiple sessions a week over a period of months.

My Thoughts:
I didn't know much about neurofeedback until I was introduced to it by some clients. They reported positive results from their treatments, which piqued my interest. As with many therapeutic modalities, there is the consideration of time and money. After implementing other modalities during my recovery, I decided to invest the time and money into neurofeedback as I was still having a hard time processing information after my trauma. I couldn't multitask as before, and my short-term memory was lacking. In my experience, neurofeedback was an effective treatment. My memory improved, I can multitask, and I am able to process complex information more effectively. My thought processes began to feel more like it did before the trauma.

Solution-Focused Therapy and Strength-Based Therapy

Positive psychology is the foundation of Solution-Focused Therapy and Strengths-Based Therapy. As the name states, the goal is to focus on solutions or strengths rather than dwelling on obstacles, problems or negative experiences. According to the father of Positive Psychology, Dr. Martin Seligman, we succeed more often when we focus on positive outcomes, strengths and best characteristics, rather than looking towards our weaknesses or problems.[15] Over the years, mental health has focused on illnesses rather than focusing on healthy practices. It is future-oriented, hopeful, and friendly with the goal of finding ways to motivate and sustain changes in a client's perspectives.[16]

My Thoughts:

I implement both Solution-Focused and Strength-Based therapies into my clients' treatment plans. Focusing on positive outcomes, creating hope and developing problem solving skills, helps clients gain confidence and build resilience. These skills carry over into all parts of their lives. Throughout client sessions, I work to recognize and magnify my client's strengths. This is especially important after a trauma when self-confidence has likely taken a significant hit. I want my clients to know that they can be in the driver's seat of their life plan and goals. This is important to understand that, regardless of where you are in the Storm or Clearing Phase, there is always Sunshine ahead.

Activities

1. Discuss with friends, family, and colleagues' what therapeutic modalities have worked well for them.
2. Research the modalities that you are interested in.
3. Find a therapist who specializes in the modalities you feel would work well for your therapeutic needs and set up an appointment.

Sources

1 Accelerated Resolution Therapy (ART): fast relief for trauma, anxiety, and depression — Tulip Tree Counseling. (2024, October 6) https://tuliptreecounseling.com/articles/art

2 What is Art Therapy? - American Art Therapy Association. (2024, January 17). American Art Therapy Association. https://arttherapy.org/what-is-art-therapy/

3 Raypole, C. (2024, September 20). What is Cognitive Behavioral Therapy (CBT)? Healthline. https://www.healthline.com/health/cognitive-behavioral-therapy#concepts

4 Cognitive Processing Therapy. (n.d.). Psychology Today. https://www.psychologytoday.com/us/therapy-types/cognitive-processing-therapy

5 VA.gov | Veterans Affairs. (n.d.). https://www.mentalhealth.va.gov/ptsd/cbt-ptsd.asp)

6 EMDR Therapy. Cleveland Clinic. (2024, May 1). https://my.clevelandclinic.org/health/treatments/22641-emdr-therapy

7 What is exposure therapy? (2017, July 31). https://www.apa.org. https://www.apa.org/ptsd-guideline/patients-and-families/exposure-therapy

8 U of U Health Authors & Marketing and Communication. (2023, February 16). Fast facts about ketamine for Depression. University of Utah Health | University of Utah Health. https://healthcare.utah.edu/healthfeed/2023/02/fast-facts-about-ketamine-depression

9 Greenwald, R. (2024, January 26). Massage therapy can support trauma healing. Trauma Institute &Amp; Child Trauma Institute. https://www.ticti.org/massage-therapy/

10 Hill, K. P., Gold, M. S., Nemeroff, C. B., McDonald, W., Grzenda, A., Widge, A. S., Rodriguez, C., Kraguljac, N. V., Krystal, J. H., & Carpenter, L. L. (2021). Risks and benefits of cannabis and cannabinoids in psychiatry. American Journal of Psychiatry, 179(2), 98–109. https://doi.org/10.1176/appi.ajp.2021.21030320

11 Medicinal Marijuana Association (n.d.) The ultimate marijuana and PTSD guide. https://www.medicinalmarijuanaassociation.com

12 Lpc/Mhsp, J. C. M. (2024, December 4). How narrative therapy works. Verywell Mind. https://www.verywellmind.com/narrative-therapy-4172956

13 Lindberg, S. (2023, February 14). What is talk therapy and can it help? Healthline. https://www.healthline.com/health/mental-health/talk-therapy#definition

14 Neurofeedback. (n.d.). Psychology Today. https://www.psychologytoday.com/us/therapy-types/neurofeedback

15 Ackerman, C. and Seligman,M. (2018, April 20). What is positive psychology & why is it important? PositivePsychology.com. https://positivepsychology.com/what-is-positive-psychology-definition/

16 Lutz, A. (2022, April 21). What is Solution-Focused Therapy · Solution-Focused Therapy Institute. The Institute for Solution-Focused Therapy. https://solutionfocused.net/what-is-solution-focused-therapy/

What are your thoughts from this Phase?

What would you like to change or implement moving forward?

SUNSHINE PHASE

Post-traumatic Growth

Renewal

Thriving

CHAPTER 34

GRATITUDE, TALENTS, & SERVICE

Courage to Shine

There are two ways of spreading light, to be the candle or the mirror that reflects it.

— Edith Wharton

I love to study human nature and behavior, both to understand individuals and how we interact as a larger community. Our objective is to live in the best way possible and create happiness for ourselves and those around us. There is beauty in the concept that we can bless each other. We all have unique strengths, skills, and talents that can profoundly enhance lives of others. Wouldn't it be inspiring and profound to capture, all at once, a lifetime of moments when others have touched our lives?

Gracious Awareness

Gratitude plays a significant role in overcoming the effects of trauma. Gracious awareness, or true gratitude, "comes from the heart, and allows for the right amount of gratefulness to keep us mentally healthy."[1] As you work through trauma, seeing the world in a positive light can be challenging, but it is possible. A study discussed in *The Happiness Advantage* by Shawn Achor found that people who considered themselves lucky, compared to those who felt unlucky, faced the same challenges but had more success. Gratitude creates positive outcomes, which in turn leads to more socially positive experiences, better sleep, and fewer headaches.[2] Recognizing the good people in our lives leads to overall well-being. Achor shared another study in which participants recorded three positive things each day. After just one week, participants were measurably less depressed and happier at one-, three-, and six-month evaluations. Seeing and recording things that are good in our lives gives us a boost, and as a bonus, we become better at seeing positive things.[3]

An example for me is the McDonald's drive-thru attendant who always greets me with a smile as she hands me my daily Coke. I appreciate how she shares a little of herself in a way that brightens my morning and gives my day a boost. Another example could be receiving a kind note from someone in our circle or words of encouragement from a colleague. The Quaker proverb, "Thee lift me, and I'll lift thee, and we'll ascend together," rings true. As we smile, serve, share our talents, and interact together, we lift each other and ascend together. Gratitude for one another and for the little interactions we have can go a long way in helping us heal from our traumatic events. Gratitude and happiness are interconnected. Expressing gratitude consistently induces positive emotions. Not only that, but everything improves, from our interpersonal relationships to our overall health. Finding genuine reasons to be grateful is like discovering small flecks of gold in an otherwise ordinary stream.

See It, Become It

Researchers found that watching films of heroic deeds that lessen suffering activates the parasympathetic nervous system, which is the body's calming response. This inspires awe and fosters admiration of those performing heroic acts. Simply put, watching someone relieve another's suffering releases feel-good chemicals in the brain, like dopamine and oxytocin. We learn best from seeing others do good things. Witnessing another human being demonstrate kindness, patience, or any type of altruistic behavior influences three different people—the person helping, the person being helped, and any witnesses. Even in their different roles, each person experiences a neurological boost of happy dopamine.[4]

Finding Courage

Helping others requires courage. It takes courage to offer kind words to a colleague or step on stage to share musical talents. Sharing our gifts, whether through acts of kindness or creative expression is contagious. These expressions of generosity spark new thoughts and inspire others to give, serve, and create as well. You can hardly attend a concert without feeling uplifted by the music and the generosity of the performers. To get on a stage and share your hard work and talents is no small feat. The willingness to be vulnerable brings out the best in all of us. (*See Chapter 36, "It only takes twenty seconds of insane courage."* [5])

Throughout the project of writing this book, I've loved the contributions from my kids and also Teresa (who is dying right now, because she'd rather be in the background) as they have shared their talents in writing, business, art, tech, design, and loving support. Their contributions naturally flow into the experience of those who read the book. It is a small sample of how humans can bless and sustain each other. I love that part of the human story!

When you've experienced trauma, it can make sharing your gifts and talents nearly impossible. I am not suggesting you step up on stage or become a performer. But what I've learned through my journey is that even a kind word or a smile—the smallest of things—can lift us and those around us.

Imagine how different the world would be if no one were brave enough to develop and share their talents. The world would feel lonely and dull. Writing this book has been a great deal of work for me and Teresa, stretching us well beyond our comfort zone. Of course, we question our abilities and whether the book will make an impact. What we are confident in, however, is that we have felt drawn to share our knowledge and experiences. If this book only helps one individual during their healing, then it will be worth it.

As I write today, I feel grateful for the teachers who've taught me, the medical professionals who went through years of schooling to help my family through health challenges. I appreciate those who've created and developed the airplanes allowing me to visit family and friends and explore the world. I even think of the brave souls who create fireworks, adding beauty to celebrations. The way we bless each other's lives and show up makes this life journey a little easier for everyone.

You never know who your talents or gifts will lift. Teresa attended physical therapy off and on over the years for a chronic condition. During one of her visits, she heard music—not through the usual overhead speaker, but live music, vibrating through the facility. Later she discovered it was the spouse of another patient. His wife, a professional musician, brought her acoustic guitar and played during his pool therapy sessions. Her music resonated throughout the entire facility quietly lifting everyone there. Her courage and willingness to share her gift became a highlight. Everyone wanted to make sure their return appointments aligned with her beautiful music. That's the power of sharing: When we share our gifts, it is a service to others. As you go through the healing process, be brave and share your art, your creativity, and your voice.

Throughout my healing experience, I have thought many times about how blessed I have been by musicians who put in the hard work and dedication to develop their talents and then were brave enough to release their music for people to listen to and judge. If there's a song that's lifted you, consider sharing it with someone else. It might be just what their hearts need today.

Connecting With Others

In the end, connecting with even one person and making a difference in that individual's life is a gift. It takes courage to share our talents, story, and skills because it exposes us to vulnerability and judgment. At times, this will feel like a win, but at others it may feel like a failure. In truth, *courage is never a failure!* One of Teresa's favorite quotes comes from Harper Lee's *To Kill A Mockingbird.* Atticus Finch says to his son Jem, "I wanted you to see what real courage is. It's when you know you're licked before you begin, but you begin anyway and see it through no matter what."[6]

Trauma can leave us feeling licked before we begin. You've come this far with me, which took courage. Courage is never failure. Sometimes, it's simply picking ourselves up and going on—no matter how it looks. Our courage today could be as simple as smiling at customers, finishing a load of laundry, making a phone call, finishing a project, keeping a promise, or making some cookies for the children. Courage doesn't have to be big, loud, or unusual. Each time we take a brave step, we are also serving and helping others through our example. Some have faced homelessness, amputations, divorce, devastating assaults, loss of a loved one, crushing defeats, or heartbreaking loss. When we're feeling fragile and overwhelmed, reading or watching inspirational stories, films, or even short clips of normal people showing compassion or generosity will positively influence our minds. Little by little, we will be brave enough to go on. We can. We will. That's why we are walking together on this journey. I'll lift thee and thee lift me, and we'll ascend together.

Activities

1. Start a daily gratitude journal, record three reasons why you are grateful every day.
2. Take a small risk to develop or share a talent.
3. Make eye contact and smile with three people throughout the day.

Sources

1. Davis, S. (2021, November 15). *Complex trauma, false gratitude, and letting go | CPTSDfoundation.org*. https://cptsdfoundation.org/2021/11/15/complex-trauma-false-gratitude-and-letting-go/
2. Achor, S. (2011b). *The happiness advantage: The Seven Principles of Positive Psychology that Fuel Success and Performance at Work*. Random House. pp. 98-100.
3. Achor, S. (2011b). *The happiness advantage: The Seven Principles of Positive Psychology that Fuel Success and Performance at Work*. Random House. p. 101.
4. Pandika, M. (n.d.). *How witnessing acts of kindness benefit our brains | U-M LSA Department of Psychology*. Retrieved February 6, 2025, from https://lsa.umich.edu/psych/news-events/all-news/faculty-news/how-witnessing-acts-of-kindness-benefit-our-brains.html
5. Mee, B. (n.d.) Quotes by Benjamin Mee. Goodreads. https://www.goodreads.com/author/quotes/1350576. Benjamin Mee
6. Lee, H. (1960). To Kill a Mockingbird. p. 128.

CHAPTER 35

POSITIVE PSYCHOLOGY

The Path to Greener Pastures

The good life is a process, not a state of being.

— Carl Rogers

After trauma, seeing the words "positive psychology" may make you think, "I'm positive I don't want to read about this." Still, I encourage you to trust me and keep reading.

As a horse rider, I know that my attention affects my horse. When riding, horses naturally follow cues from their rider. It is crucial that as a rider, your eyes stay focused on where you want the horse to go. Shifting your attention can confuse the horse. If you look down, the horse may stop. If you turn and look behind you, the horse may follow your gaze and turn with you.

A middle-aged man decided to ride a horse for the first time. The horse was gentle and obedient, making it a good choice for a beginner. As he grew confident riding around the small grassy pasture, he nudged the horse into a light gallop. As the horse went faster, the rider became fixated on a telephone pole at the edge of the pasture. The bystanders, who were experienced riders, understood what was about to happen and started to shout, "Turn! Don't look at the pole! Look away—Turn!" All the warnings failed; the inexperienced rider galloped the horse directly into the telephone pole.

The pasture was wide open. The telephone pole stood off to the side, and frankly, it was difficult to hit. What happened? Rather than looking towards the open field or a better path, the rider became focused on missing the telephone pole–the place he did not want to go.

The focus and training used in riding translates well into positive psychology. Focusing on the wrong obstacle can bring unnecessary hard knocks. The target of our mental focus can define our path or the direction we go. Influential figures like Shawn Achor and Martin Seligman were instrumental trailblazers in directing research and therapists' attention to positive psychology. Positive psychology is defined as "the scientific study of strengths that enable individuals and communities to thrive."[1] It involves identifying distorted or misleading thought patterns associated with anxiety and depression. Think of them as mental telephone poles—unnecessary and potentially harmful. They serve no purpose. There is no practical need to focus on them. What was true on one occasion will not always be true for the rest of our lives. Just because you ran one red light does not mean you will run every red light for the rest of your life. Just because we have failed or had a negative experience in the past does not mean we will continue to fail in the future. Our past does not define who we are. By changing our thought processes, we can change our lives. Our mistakes or negative experiences can become telephone poles. If we keep looking at them, we may drive into them again and again. Positive psychology helps us change our focus and see the bigger and greener pastures surrounding us.

Shawn Achor, happiness researcher, speaker, and author of international best-seller, *The Happiness Advantage* –one of my favorite books—reveals that focusing on thoughts or experiences that bring laughter and joy can improve outcomes. You may have believed that happiness is a result of achievements, such as winning a contract or being awarded a new job, a raise, a car, an outfit, or other tangible rewards. According to Achor, research shows otherwise. Simple things like a small treat, a happy memory, or a humorous video clip can relieve stress, increase test scores, and even influence doctors to make more accurate diagnoses.[2] We've all been in tense situations when someone says something unexpectedly hilarious. The tension breaks, laughter follows, and everyone feels better.

Moreover, intentionally shifting our thoughts and behavior toward happiness can lead to greater emotional well-being. What our minds believe, we enact. Our beliefs define our reality, changing our physical, mental, and emotional well-being for better or worse.[3]

A recent, large-scale, multi-laboratory international study published in *Nature Human Behaviour* demonstrated that our emotions are affected by our physical actions. The act of smiling, even if it's a fake smile, can increase happiness. Dr. Nicholas Coles, of *Stanford University*, concluded that whenever we activate our smile muscles it positively affects our perceptions and emotions. We can influence our minds into feeling happier just by smiling.[4]

Studies have shown a single negative experience can have up to five times the impact of a positive one. It may take five positive thoughts to counteract the emotional and physical influence of one negative thought. While many traumatic experiences are the result of others' choices or actions, focusing on blame is especially destructive. Negative thoughts allow the trauma to continuously reinforce your role as a victim, thereby blocking healing.

Researchers have recently recognized that there are multiple effective coping styles. However, the most effective approaches are rooted in positive strategies. Positivity helps heal the brain and move forward from trauma.[5]

Research suggests several different ways we can refocus our thoughts:

- Using encouraging words
- Taking a walk
- Watching a short clip of a comedian
- Reviewing our positive traits and strengths
- Envisioning a meaningful goal—large or small

These activities and others can reduce stress and refocus our minds on more positive, productive, and hopeful thoughts.[6]

Achor suggests that simple acts such as serving others or using a forgotten skill or talent will give us a spark of positivity and boost happiness. Contemplating or daydreaming about a relaxing experience or a favorite pastime can infuse our minds with positive endorphins. Looking forward to activities like visiting a favorite restaurant, seeing a new show, attending a music festival, can increase our happy endorphins. The mere act of anticipating a positive experience raises our happy hormones. Other ways to enrich our lives with positivity include physical activity and exercise. They have been shown to effectively lift mood, reduce stress and alleviate anxiety.[7] I use positive psychology in my practice. It fosters an intentional mindset focused on creating joy, practicing gratitude, and having fun.

In J.M. Barrie's original *Peter Pan* play, Wendy, John, and Michael are taught that mixing "lovely, wonderful thoughts" with fairy dust would make them light enough to fly.[8] Can our thoughts really make our challenges lighter? Negative thoughts and events have a greater emotional impact than positive ones, and intentional changes are required to remove negative and destructive thinking patterns. Negative thought patterns, like blame or self-reproach, are devastating. In some interesting studies, researchers found that both mindset and social support influence how individuals perceive physical challenges. In one study, individuals with a negative mindset perceived a steep hill to be 30 percent steeper than it actually was. Those who face the climb alone overestimated the incline to be 20 percent steeper compared to those who had a friend nearby.[9] Simply put, if you are facing difficult challenges, keep a friend nearby and intentionally think positive thoughts, and the challenge, no matter how difficult, will appear easier.

Positive psychology is life-changing, and as we work on thinking lovely, wonderful thoughts, we will all find paths to something better than some ugly old telephone pole. Should you get caught in a cycle of negative thinking, remember the telephone pole! There's no reason for you or me to focus on the telephone poles of our negative thoughts. They serve no purpose for us. We can avoid them by shifting our attention better directions. Focus on anything else—food, fun, serving others, creating art, cleaning a corner that's driving you nuts, or recalling happy memories. Don't accidentally focus on the telephone pole or negative thoughts and get hurt. As soon as you see a negative thought coming your way, intentionally turn your focus somewhere else.

After my traumatic experience, I had to make an intentional effort every single day to look towards greener pastures rather than focus on a negative telephone pole. While it is not an easy shift, it is possible. Trauma can carry so much sadness, fear, anger, and darkness. We may need to sit with these emotions for a while, understand them, and process them in a healthy way. Ultimately, the goal is to work through the pain, grief and other important emotions. The next step is to intentionally guide our thoughts toward a positive mindset, which allows us to direct our future.

The undeniable truth is I want to live a joyful, peaceful life. I want to see my world in a bright, happy yellow—my favorite color—not out of denial or naivete, but because we are meant to enjoy life. Life is full of painful experiences and hard events, but I desire a more joyful, fun, and peaceful life despite the hard parts. I refuse to let a traumatic experience steal that from me. No matter what happens to us, we oversee our story and how we live it.

After my trauma *Storm* and in the midst of the *Clearing Phase* I realized I faced a decision every morning. I could focus on telephone pole-like obstacles like the unfairness of life, the hurt and sadness, and the overwhelming challenges ahead—or I could shift my brain to focus on the larger, greener pasture. I could purposefully identify good things in my life, the obstacles I could overcome, the new skills I could learn, and new goals I could work towards. I could learn to achieve my goals and muster the courage to experience new things. I could see all that was right and good in my life. I was in the driver's seat. One of my new goals on my vision board was to write a book. The negative thoughts fought back: "*You're not skilled enough. You're not a writer. No one will care.*" I countered with intentional positive thoughts: "*You can learn. Your story matters. Helping even one person makes it worthwhile.*" One line of thought leads me to the telephone pole while the other opens me up to a beautiful field filled with possibilities.

As a therapist, there is no greater reward than witnessing a client shift as they learn how to use an intentional positive mindset to stop focusing on the telephone poles in their lives. It takes effort, but as they have focused on their strengths, their capabilities, their courage, creating joy, finding gratitude, having fun, and thinking wonderful thoughts, they become better at guiding their thoughts away from the negative, allowing them to see the world differently and find happiness and joy. They feel more powerful and hold the pen to write their story. Like Wendy, John, and Michael, from Peter Pan, as we begin to think intentionally happy or lovely thoughts, a form of magic appears, and it's wonderful to witness a client, friend, or family member see positive possibilities and watch them become light enough to fly on their own and create their own path and journey in powerful ways even they didn't expect.

Activities

1. Think of a difficult or painful experience (telephone pole) from your past. Imagine how life could look if that moment no longer held power over your identity. Continue to read books related to Positive Psychology to learn how to intergrate the concept into your life.
2. Imagine a meaningful goal—big or small—that brings a sense of hope or excitement:
    - *Write about why this matters to you.*
    - *List small steps you could take towards it.*
    - *Think about how you feel now that you are focusing on something hopeful.*
3. Make of list of happy experiences or things that bring a smile to your face: review them daily.

Additional Resources

- *The Happiness Lab* podcast with Dr. Laurie Santos
- *Happier* podcast with Gretchen Rubin
- *The Science of Happiness* by Greater Good Science Center
- *The Happiness Advantage* by Shawn Achor

Sources

1 *Our mission | Positive Psychology Center.* (n.d.-b). https://ppc.sas.upenn.edu/our-mission

2 Achor, S. (2011b). *The happiness advantage: The Seven Principles of Positive Psychology that Fuel Success and Performance at Work.* Random House. pp.46-49.

3 *The Happiness Advantage.* p.71

4 Jeffay, N. (2022, October 22). Even if faked smiling make you feel happier huge international study finds. *Times of Israel.* https://www.timesofisrael.com/even-if-faked-smiling-makes-you-feel-happier-huge-international-study-finds/

5 Timms, M. (2022) *Blame culture is toxic. Here's how to stop it. (2022, February 11). Harvard Business Review. https://hbr.org/2022/02/blame-culture-is-toxic-heres-how-to-stop-it*

6 *The Happiness Advantage.* pp. 46-49

7 *The Happiness Advantage.* pp.52-57

8 Lowne, C., & Bauer, P. (2025, January 9). *Peter Pan | Plot, analysis, Characters, & Facts.* Encyclopedia Britannica. https://www.britannica.com/topic/Peter-Pan-play-by-Barrie

9 Schnall, S., Harber, K. D., Stefanucci, J. K., Proffitt, D. R., University of Plymouth, Department of Psychology, Rutgers University at Newark, Department of Psychology, The College of William and Mary, & Department of Psychology, University of Virginia. (2008). Social support and the perception of geographical slant. In *Journal of Experimental Social Psychology* (Vol. 44, pp. 1246–1255) [Journal-article]. http://nwkpsych.rutgers.edu/~kharber/publications/Schnall.et.al.2008.Social%20Support%20and%20the%20Perception%20of%20Geographical%20Slant.pdf

CHAPTER 36

RESILIENCE & POST-TRAUMATIC GROWTH

Surviving to Thriving, I Like the New Me

True transformation is an inner journey,
where self-awareness leads to growth and resilience leads to breakthrough.

— Anonymous

The growth that arises from trauma can be transformative. It is inspiring to watch clients who have felt broken evolve through the *Trauma Impact Phases,* from *Storm,* to *Clearing,* and eventually to *Sunshine.* As they find their way, putting one foot in front of the other, they become stronger and continue to grow. Clinically this is called post-traumatic growth. Observing their strength and their personal, life-changing growth after trauma is uplifting and reaffirms the resilience of the human spirit.

I've had the honor of guiding clients through some inspiring transformations. Whether someone battling severe depression and finding joy, someone being paralyzed by anxiety taking on the world again, or a girl sexually assulted learning to see their worth, the process is profound. Watching clients move from chronic suffering to flourishing after therapy is like the awe of seeing a double rainbow after a storm. It's the kind of beauty you don't expect to witness in the midst of hardship. These transformations are deeply moving — clients with chronic or terminal conditions embracing life fully, survivors of abuse becoming confident entrepreneurs, or widows reclaiming their joy and independence.

Working through trauma presents challenges. It brings countless tears, heartache, pain, and vulnerability, all of which requires immense effort. There is only one way to get to the other side of trauma to see the brightness of hope and light breaking through – that is to go through the pain and healing process. When the sun shines a light on the growth and beauty, it is an "aha" moment as resilience and courage triumph. As we fight not only to survive but to thrive, we will experience enlightenment and new horizons in our lives.

Resilience

Since I was a little girl, I have been in awe of Joan of Arc's strength, and bravery, along with Florence Nightingale's compassion and courage. Their unwavering courage and strength illuminated my thoughts, because I wanted to be like them when I grew up. As a child, I could not understand that such strength often comes from surviving trauma. Although details of Joan of Arc's life are limited, her ability to stand firm in the face of daunting obstacles remains extraordinary. At just sixteen, Joan of Arc became a national hero in France, displaying remarkable bravery and resilience. She led the French army to victory in the 1400s, forcing the English to abandon their siege.[1]

Florence Nightingale was a brave pioneer, often referred to as the founder of modern nursing. A force to be reckoned with, Florence demonstrated incredible leadership and fortitude during the 1854 Crimean War by organizing nurses to care for wounded soldiers under horrific conditions.[2]

Harvard human performance researcher Marcus Buckingham teaches, "We discover our resilience only when we are forced to meet unavoidable suffering full in the face. It's when we face that reality, and see ourselves and how we respond to it, that we find the basis for resilience."[3]

We see courage and resilience throughout history, but also in everyday life—in ourselves and in those around us. As we face our own struggles, we discover strength in ourselves —strength we didn't know existed. The *American Psychological Association (APA)* defines resilience as "the process and outcome of successfully adapting to difficult or life-changing life experiences."[4] Resilience comes as we learn to cope with trauma. Moving from the *Clearing Phase* to the *Sunshine Phase,* each day becomes a conscious choice to live with courage. Each new day faced with intention builds courage and strengthen in our coping skills. British author Benjamin Mee wrote about his courageous journey in his 2008 memoir, *We Bought a Zoo*. He shares his philosophy of resilience and courage: "You know, sometimes all you need is twenty seconds of insane courage. Just literally twenty seconds of embarrassing bravery. And I promise you, something great will come of it."[5]

Post-traumatic Growth

The idea of post-traumatic growth comes from psychologists Richard Tedeschi and Lawrence Calhoun and refers to finding ways to continue to grow after trauma, leading to more resilience and an increased understanding of and appreciation for ourselves and those around us, our life, and the world we live in.

American Psychological Association (APA) writer Lorna Collier specified the five areas where Tedeschi and Calhoun look for positive growth:

- Appreciation of life
- Relationships with others
- New possibilities in life
- Personal strength
- Spiritual change[6]

As my post-traumatic growth has unfolded, I am not the same person I was before. While many aspects remain the same, a new version of myself has emerged. This one is more resilient, appreciative of life, and stronger. Adding to that, I have a deeper understanding of what it takes to do hard things.

I am a survivor and have faith. I can trust my judgment. In my growth process, I have gained greater empathy for others and have learned to value happiness and embrace calmness more than ever before. Relationships are dear to me, and I have an increased commitment to center my life in peace and joy. Most of all, I now know that I will be okay and that I am resilient.

Growing from surviving to thriving, I have come to realize *I like the new version of me!*

Activities

1. Write down attributes and growth you see in yourself.
2. Identify times in your past you have seen strength and resilience in your life.
3. Can you see growth in the specific areas of: appreciation of life, relationships with others, new possibilities in life, personal strength, spiritual change?

Sources

1 Vale, M. G., & Lanhers, Y. (2025, January 7). *Joan of Arc | Biography, death, accomplishments, & Facts.* Encyclopedia Britannica. https://www.britannica.com/biography/Saint-Joan-of-Arc

2 *Florence Nightingale's story and legacy | British Red Cross.* (2023). British Red Cross. https://www.redcross.org.uk/stories/health-and-social-care/health/how-florence-nightingale-influenced-the-red-cross

3 *Buckingham, M. (2021b, August 30). What really makes us resilient? Harvard Business Review. https://hbr.org/2020/09/what-really-makes-us-resilient*

4 Laderer, A. (2023, November 2). Trauma Resilience: What it is and how to build it. *Charlie Health.*

5 Mee, B. (n.d.) Quotes by Benjamin Mee. Goodreads. https://www.goodreads.com/author/quotes/1350576. Benjamin Mee

6 Collier, L. (2016). *Growth after trauma.* https://www.apa.org. November 2016, Vol 47, No. 10. Print version: page 48 https://www.apa.org/monitor/2016/11/growth-trauma

CHAPTER 37

REDEFINING & RENEWING STRENGTHS

Blooming and Flourishing

Life tried to crush her but only succeeded in making a diamond.

—John Mark Green

After a traumatic experience, we may ask, "Who am I?" Trauma can remove the boundaries that once defined us, leading to an existential crisis as we question and consider our real identity.

Teresa shares her experience:

One clear spring day, I was driving homeward when a question popped into my mind: "Who are you?"

I spoke to myself listing my roles, "I am a mother, a volunteer, a teacher, a pianist, a bookkeeper."

The quiet voice in my mind countered bluntly, "That's what you do, that is not who you are. Who are you?"

For the next few nights, as I lay awake, the question haunted me, and for good reason.

Loss of Independence

Later that same year, I developed what initially seemed like a routine infection. When it didn't clear up, a week passed, then two, then a month, and then more. Despite my hopes, there was no improvement and over time, my condition worsened. Week after week, I was forced to cancel another commitment. The undiagnosed illness not only changed my life but also upended my little family's world. It took months to find answers and then years to rebuild my strength. The only thing that was clear was instead of being a caregiver and always on the go, I needed to be cared for.

Every task, and all my responsibilities physically and mentally became a struggle. I could barely lift up my feet, and felt as if my arms and legs were made of cement. Normal things like combing my hair and cooking dinner felt impossible.

My children, ages 8-13, became my biggest cheerleaders and helpers. As a mother, changing my role from the caregiver to the receiver of care was humiliating and frustrating, but at the same time, I was immensely grateful to be surrounded by my children, my husband, and so many caring, helpful people.

One day, a kind neighbor who lived a few blocks away kept my children for the afternoon, allowing me to rest. When my husband came home, I tried to explain that he needed to bring the kids back, frustration took over as I couldn't say what I meant. Finally, we climbed into the car and I pointed the way until we arrived at the correct neighbor's home. It was a scary low point—going from functioning as a perfectly normal human to this drastic change. Everything was difficult—grocery shopping, finances, scheduling—it all felt impossible. I expected life as usual and my strength to return the next day. It did not.

We decided we needed to move to a house that was easier for me to get around in. With my limited ability to drive, I was forced to depend on others for help. It was uncomfortable to ask for help. My family and I missed our old friends, schools, and the happy life we loved. The activities, the community, and the busy schedule of sports and volunteering...everything was gone. Our comfortable world was lost, and so was my confidence.

Thinking back to the question, "Who are you?", I realized none of my original answers remained in my life—other than being a wife and mother. While I didn't understand at the time, this is often the case with any type of trauma. Everything we once knew can become uncertain or wiped out. As youth leader Michelle Craig explained, this type of change challenged everything, including my faith, my family, and my future.[1]

A neurologist asked me, "How are you doing outside of your health?" He encouraged me to find a new sense of purpose in my life, something beyond my health struggles. His words, though brief, gave me courage and strength to start thinking about my life differently. Rebuilding the exact life and person I used to be was not realistic. Like so many others who've endured a catastrophic change in their lives, I had to discover new strengths, create new goals, and realize that the life I had would never return.

Should anyone ask me now, "Who are you?", my answer is, "I hope I am someone who makes you laugh."

When Teresa became ill, she had to redefine her gifts, her strengths, and also her goals. It was a life-changing experience that forced her to question her identity and purpose. Unfortunately, painful or traumatic experiences change us more than happy experiences and can force us to question everything.[2] The defining boundaries we are accustomed to can be moved, causing an existential crisis that leaves us wondering who we are.

Logic or Fear?

After my own *Storm Phase* of trauma, even though I didn't have a medical event like Teresa, my body felt fatigued, my mind was foggy, and everything ached. In the blur of the chaos created by the traumatic experience, I felt paralyzed and blocked, doubting my abilities. Though I had tangible evidence of strengths I had once applied in my life, it now felt as if those strengths belonged to someone else, not me. Confusing thoughts and fear collided through my consciousness. One part clung to logic, while the other was full of doubts and uncertainty. I was stunned and wondered how this traumatic experience could break my brain and push me to question so much that I had previously understood to be true about myself.

In the past, I was a resilient problem solver and a productive multitasker, full of confidence. I'd carried responsibility well and accomplished difficult things, earning the nickname "Grace Under Fire."

As I moved from the trauma *Storm Phase* and into the *Clearing Phase*, it was as though my past accomplishments and abilities had been wiped out. My confidence was gone. My inner strength was shaken, causing me to question if confidence and strength ever existed at all. Like so many others who've been through trauma *Storms,* I wondered if I would ever feel strong again. The back and forth of my thoughts was like a pendulum. I understood my doubts and fears were not entirely accurate. My personal and professional experiences had shown me otherwise. I knew individuals could heal from trauma and not only survive, but thrive. I had to keep my eye on this knowledge and have hope that this could be my story too. And it was!

Activities

1. Make a list of strengths you have relied upon in the past.
2. Visit the sites: *insightfultraits.com* and/or *Authentic Happiness* website and take the free signature strengths test.
3. Listen to the podcast *Practically Happy with Miranda Anderson #309: What are your Signature Strengths.*

Sources

1 Craig, B. S. M. D. (2022, October 1). *Wholehearted.* https://www.churchofjesuschrist.org/study/general-conference/2022/10/32craig?lang=eng

2 Barber, N., PhD. (2012, December 13). Traumatic events as "deep" as personality. *Psychology Today.* https://www.psychologytoday.com/us/blog/the-human-beast/201212/trauma-resets-personality

CHAPTER 38

FORGIVENESS

Setting Ourselves Free

To forgive is to set a prisoner free and discover that the prisoner was you.

— Lewis B. Smedes

Challenges of Forgiveness

It is easy to feel burdened or guilty when we hear stories of people who forgive immediately. It is also easy to misjudge people who forgive easily as naive, unrealistic, or detached from reality. But what would be the point of this journey if we did not at least gain wisdom? One piece of wisdom we gain is to be gentle with ourselves and others as we process and work through our emotions. As we work through the *Trauma Impact Phases,* there is no reason to judge ourselves or others harshly—especially when it comes to forgiveness.

Like everything in this healing journey, the decision to forgive and the timing of forgiveness is personal and different for everyone. This can be challenging, especially since nearly every major religion teaches forgiveness as a main tenet of faith and that it is wrong to harbor hatred:

Qur'an 64:14

But if you pardon and overlook and forgive—then indeed, Allah is Forgiving and Merciful

Leviticus 19:18, KJV

Thou shalt not avenge, nor bear any grudge against the children of thy people, but thou shalt love thy neighbor as thyself

Guru Granth Sahib, Ang 1374

Forgiveness is the virtue of the brave, and one who forgives is liberated

Doctrine and Covenants 64:9-11

I, the Lord will forgive whom I will forgive, but of you, it is required to forgive all men

Beyond the spiritual meaning, the act of forgiveness is beneficial in other ways. Psychiatrist Karen Swartz explains, "There is an enormous physical burden to being hurt and disappointed." Resentment, outrage, and chronic anger cause changes that can negatively impact physical health by increasing depression, heart disease, and other inflammatory diseases like diabetes. Forgiveness, however, can have a positive impact on overall health, including reducing depression and pain while improving sleep and other stress-related symptoms. Interestingly enough, the correlation between forgiveness and good health grows stronger as we age.[1]

While I am fully aware of the health benefits of forgiveness and the spiritual foundations behind it, some clients still ask if it is *really* necessary. The answer is that forgiveness can protect you from further emotional and physical damage. *But how is it done?* Especially in situations where the offender who caused the trauma deflects, avoids, shifts the blame, or seems oblivious to the consequences, forgiveness becomes even more difficult. The challenge in forgiving becomes even more painful when the legal system fails to hold the offender accountable, deepening the pain. This has been the case for many women who have been sexually assaulted or people who have experienced the emotional toll of divorcing someone displaying narcissistic traits. Alternatively, the offender may have greater access to resources or finances for legal fees. Forgiveness does not give anyone permission to harm you again. Forgiveness should never be rushed — especially during the

Storm Phase, when emotions are raw, and survival takes priority. Finding safety and gaining a clearer mindset is the first step. To someone recovering from trauma while also having to deal with civil or criminal legal matters, forgiveness may take much longer.

Forgiveness is NOT Permission

Forgiveness does not mean putting ourselves in toxic and abusive relationships, excusing offenses, or blaming ourselves for others' actions or choices. What it does mean is that we don't give the offender the power to create darkness within us. Forgiving is working toward peace and joy while intentionally removing the desire for revenge from our hearts. *John Hopkins Medicine* warns that when people feel forced or manipulated into forgiving someone to salvage a relationship, the relationship actually worsens.[2] Forgiveness must be given freely on your timeline, as part of healthy healing. It should never be forced, coerced, or demanded.

A friend's mother used to tell her all the time when she was young, "Don't you worry, God will get them." Forgiveness was often mixed with messages of revenge, blurring the concept of forgiveness. She was told that forgiveness was virtuous, and that God would take care of justice. She was also told that revenge was an honorable responsibility. The contradiction left her struggling to understand the meaning of forgiveness. As an adult, she reformed her own definition of forgiveness. Eventually, she shared her thoughts with me:

Forgiveness is not:

- *Forgiveness is not something that you should feel forced or coerced into*
- *Forgiveness is not accepting, promoting, or permitting poor behavior*
- *Forgiveness is not excusing damaging behavior*
- *Forgiveness is not taking responsibility for another's actions*
- *Forgiveness does not mean reconciliation*
- *Forgiveness does not mean wishing God will repay them (That's still revenge)*

- *Forgiveness does not depend on being "asked" for forgiveness*[3]
- *Forgiveness does not have to include a full pardon or second opportunity (While it can in certain circumstances, pardoning or allowing a second chance is never required)*

Forgiveness is:

- *Forgiveness is an intentional choice*
- *Forgiveness is given freely without any expectations*
- *Forgiveness is a deliberate choice that brings relief to our heavy hearts*
- *Forgiveness is letting go of the desire for resentment, hostility, bitterness, retribution, or revenge*
- *Forgiveness is giving something undeserved to another.*
- *Forgiveness is giving space for peace.*[4]

Mary Johnson's only son, 20-year-old Laramiun Byrd, was killed by an act of violence. Mary shared her philosophy in a CBS News interview, saying, "Unforgiveness is like cancer, it will eat you from the inside out. It's not about the other person. Me forgiving him does not diminish what he's done. Yes, he murdered my son, but *the forgiveness is for me. It's for me.*"[5]

Mary realized that holding onto negative emotions was not in her best interest. In her case, time and forgiveness led—unexpectedly—to a relationship with the young man who had taken her son's life. She did not begin with the intention to build a friendship. Although in deep pain and suffering, she found peace in supporting him. Forgiveness plays a complex and often surprising role in the trauma recovery journey. Letting go of resentment, hurt, and hatred is especially difficult when the trauma is caused by others, and we still need to shield and protect ourselves from further harm.

Jackpots and Tender Mercies

Positive reinforcement expert and animal behavior trainer Karen Pryor explained how forgiveness changed her life. As an adolescent, she was stubborn, unhappy and disagreeable. Her father and stepmother explained they were going to do something about her behavior, and rather than scold her or give her what she deserved, they surprised her with the one thing she valued above anything else in her life at that time—a ticket for horseback riding lessons. It's something she had neither earned nor deserved. Karen called these unearned rewards, such as her riding ticket, a "jackpot" in the training world.[6] When we give others something unexpected or undeserved, it changes the giver and very often the heart of the receiver. In my faith, we refer to such an act as "a tender mercy."[7] Giving forgiveness when it is neither deserved nor earned changes us, and often it will change the person you are forgiving. In Mary Johnson's case, her forgiveness transformed the life of the young man who took her son's life. Today, they live next to each other and share a close, meaningful relationship. When we forgive, we find healing, hope, and peace.[8]

A Nation's Example of Forgiveness

In 2006, the Amish community was changed by a man who entered a Pennsylvania school and took the lives of five innocent children while wounding five others. This tragedy gripped the attention of a nation as we observed the Amish community forgive the shooter. Parents in their deepest moments of grief offered tender mercies to his family. In the earliest days following this heartbreaking event, they offered their forgiveness and even raised money to support his family. As a community and as individuals, they still had to live with the trauma, shock, and emotional damage done to their children and community. But their willingness to forgive the offender and embrace his family gave them the grace to move forward.[9] Forgiveness is not about the person who caused the harm. When a person grants forgiveness, it frees them from the damage of holding on to hate, and they can focus on healing.[10] In my trauma recovery, I have intentionally been working on focusing on my healing rather than hate or negative feelings. *It is not easy.* It is painful, but it is the best way to move forward and reclaim your life after a traumatic experience.

The Challenges of Forgiving Ourselves

The question, "How do I forgive them?" surfaces frequently in my practice. Another common question is, "How do I forgive myself?" Without oversimplifying, forgiveness begins with a decision. It starts by saying, "I have decided to find peace and remove the chains of anger, injustice, resentment, or other toxic emotions." In my work with clients, we discuss how changing our mindset can change our path. This intentional change helps us shift into new ways, new thoughts, and new light. It is a conscientious, deliberate, and purposeful process. Some questions to consider when we want to forgive, but it feels too difficult:

- *What do I gain by not forgiving myself?*
- *What do I gain by holding on to the anger or hate?*
- *What would life look like if I forgave myself and others?*

Moving Forward

Mary Johnson did not know what challenges she faced when she chose to forgive. Similarly, the Amish community of Nickel Mines, Pennsylvania did not know the difficulties they would encounter when they made the decision to forgive. Despite the challenges, they made a decision. When we are ready to forgive and find peace, our decision becomes our guide. As thoughts of anger arise, we counteract them with the commitment we made: "I want to forgive." As feelings of anger start to creep in, this is when we remind ourselves of our desire for peace. With patience and time, forgiveness will come. It has the power to transform our lives and the lives of everyone we interact with.

Holding onto anger—toward ourselves or others—can keep us ensnared in a victim mindset, complicating the process of forgiveness. There can be a sharp conflict between what our minds and beliefs tell us we should do and the deep hurt, pain, or disgust we still feel. How can we forgive when we have been hurt by another's actions or when someone we love has been harmed?

Forgiveness can be even more challenging when someone we love has been hurt. Personal pain is different from watching someone else suffer. Talking about forgiveness is one thing; putting it into effect takes practice and doesn't come easily. For me, the journey began with my own experiences of trauma caused by others' choices and behaviors. I've spent a lifetime working through this, starting with letting go of anger and bitterness toward my birth father for abandoning our family. My journey in finding peace in the forgiveness process has been a combination of religious studies and working through my heightened emotions with EMDR therapy. As my belief system incorporates the teachings of Jesus Christ, in meditation and prayer I ask Him to take the chains and heavy rocks I am carrying and imagine laying them at His feet. This image is powerful for me. Others with different belief systems will have a variety of sources that can aid in their forgiveness journey. I encourage you to create an image that you practice in your mind of taking off the chains and unloading the heavy rocks you are carrying.

I still have space for continued growth in learning to forgive and perhaps it will be a lifetime of work as it can feel challenging at times. It is my desire though, so I am putting intentional effort into the process. Please remember that we each have our own timeframe and don't need to subscribe to what others think should be our path of forgiveness. Be kind to yourself and patient with the process.

Forgiveness is a choice, but it doesn't eliminate all the difficulties of a trauma journey. It allows us to move forward by setting down some of the heavier burdens we've been carrying. Witnessing others' ability to forgive can inspire and guide us in our own journey. I recommend exploring podcasts, books, support groups, and internet sources such as *The Forgiveness Project*[11] or *The F Word Podcast* (the F stands for forgiveness) for stories of how forgiveness can transform, mend, and help us face the most challenging and traumatic events.

Activities

1. Spend some time considering how you view forgiveness.
2. Look for a story about forgiveness that you find inspiring.
3. Is there a grudge or anger you hold towards yourself or someone else? How would life look if you forgave yourself? How would life look if you forgave someone else?

Additional Resources

- Stories on forgiveness can be found at: www.theforgivenessproject.com
- *The F Word Podcast* podcast by Marina Cantacuzino
- *Love, Forgive, Live* podcast by Sroda Agalgoh
- *Project Forgiveness* by Bobbie Frye

Sources

1 John Hopkins Medicine: Health. (n.d.) *Forgiveness: Your Health Depends on It.* (n.d.). Retrieved January 27, 2025, from https://www.hopkinsmedicine.org/health/wellness-and-prevention/forgiveness-your-health-depends-on-it

2 John Hopkins Medical, Health. (n.d.) *Forgiveness: Your Health Depends on It.* (n.d.). Retrieved January 27, 2025, from https://www.hopkinsmedicine.org/health/wellness-and-prevention/forgiveness-your-health-depends-on-it

3 Kupisk, D. (2020, November 5). *Finding Forgiveness: How to practice and model forgiveness.* Parenthetical. https://parenthetical.wisc.edu/2018/06/05/finding-forgiveness-how-to-practice-and-model-forgiveness/

4 Kearl, T. (2024) Personal Experience.

5 CBS News, & Johnson, M. (2011, June 7). *The power of forgiveness* [Video]. YouTube. https://www.youtube.com/watch?v=o2BITY-3Mp4. Emphasis added.

6 Pryor, K. (1999). *Don't shoot the dog! The New Art of Teaching and Training.* pp11-13. Bantam.

7 Psalm 25:6, KJV

8 Lyubomirsky, S., Sheldon, K. M., & Schkade, D. (2005). Pursuing Happiness: The architecture of sustainable change. *Review of General Psychology, 9*(2), 111–131. https://doi.org/10.1037/1089-2680.9.2.111

9 Kraybill, D. B., Nolt, S. M., & Weaver-Zercher, D. L. (2007). *Amish grace: How forgiveness transcended tragedy.* Jossey-Bass.

10 Shapiro, J. (2007, October 2). Amish Forgive School Shooter, Struggle with Grief. *NPR.* https://www.npr.org/2007/10/02/14900930/amish-forgive-school-shooter-struggle-with-grief

11 Richman, K. (2024, December 13). *The Forgiveness Project.* The Forgiveness Project. https://www.theforgivenessproject.com/

CHAPTER 39

CLAIMING YOUR STORY

Courage in Truth

Sharing our truths can provide the opportunity for great healing.

— Kristen Noel

Trauma impact might cause us to lose sight of who we are and shift the way we view the world. It may cause us to question our values, reevaluate our roles in relationships, see our vulnerabilities, or feel unsure of ourselves and our place in the world. It may even make us question if we can trust ourselves and others. Trauma has a way of shaking our internal self like a snow globe being turned upside down. Sometimes our trauma might include the negative actions of others—abuse, betrayal, broken promises, misjudgments, or accidents. Our stories can feel messy. Perhaps we feel shame or embarrassment or wish we had handled the situation differently. We might be cautious in sharing the story because we are concerned about hurting others. We might be uncomfortable with ourselves, have self-doubt, or fear potential consequences, judgment, or backlash.

Our experience can be hijacked by different voices, opinions, fears, and self-doubt. These factors can make us lose our authenticity, along with compromising our peace and connection to ourselves. Peace within ourselves comes through being genuine and transparent in our feelings and experiences. Rewriting or softening our experiences can prevent healing because the brain and the body keep a true record of events as they transpired. Dutch-American psychiatrist and groundbreaking expert on trauma's effects on the body, Dr. Bessel van der

Kolk, conveys a powerful insight: *"As long as you keep secrets and suppress information, you are fundamentally at war with yourself."*[1] We cannot hide from the truthfulness of the experience no matter how we may try to avoid it.

To change, people must become aware of the way their body responds to stress, emotions and surroundings. Have you found peace within your body in claiming your experiences and story? If not, what needs to be claimed, sorted out, or spoken? I refer to this internal assessment and process of necessary changes as "recalibrating," meaning to keep working through emotions and memories in order to settle the brain and body to feel at peace. I love watching this process with clients as they go from feeling out of sorts and outside of their story to settling into it and claiming it. Instead of the trauma holding the story, they hold the pen. *They control the story and trauma.* The trauma no longer controls them.

Brené Brown, an inspiring speaker, podcaster, and therapist, encourages teachers, leaders, and individuals with her powerful words, "Owning our story and loving ourselves through that process is the bravest thing we'll ever do."[2] Yes! It is a courageous process. I have witnessed many take on the challenge and find their story and peace. Owning our stories doesn't mean we have to write a book or create a blog about our stories, it simply means accepting what happened and moving forward.

No Shortcuts

Despite my knowledge and experience in this philosophy, there were no shortcuts in the hard work of embracing my story. There are many ups and downs as our brain processes the details, emotions, and as we accept the truth of how and why our world has changed. This is a recalibration of our mind, heart and body. While in the *Storm* and some of the *Clearing Phase*, I was more guarded when it came to sharing my thoughts and feelings. Looking back, I realize this fear was rooted in discomfort, confusion, and the need for protection. However, as time passed, I came to understand my story and found peace in sharing my thoughts and feelings with those around me.

When I already felt so vulnerable it was difficult to be open, but it was essential for my growth. This openness allowed me to share what I was experiencing and how it was impacting me with those I loved. "Trauma, whether it is the result of something done to you or something you yourself have done, almost always makes it difficult to engage in intimate relationships."[3] Sharing traumatic experiences might feel nearly impossible and may require support. The narrative of the story we share is about putting your thoughts, feelings and experiences into words. Sharing my story was about gaining confidence and recognizing my value. This was about recognizing my worth and accepting truth in the details. As I did so, I felt empowered.

Being empowered in a story does not mean it has to be shared; there is always a choice. As Dr. Bessel van de Kolk observed in *The Body Keeps Score,* healing begins when we reclaim our past as our own.[4] Acknowledging what our bodies are saying means we are good listeners to ourselves. What truth does your body hold? Is it craving expression, or does it find peace in silence? Sharing our stories with others can strengthen connections, offer validation, and inspire advocacy in non-profit or policy forums.

Letting the Skeletons Out

In past generations, as a society, many things were kept private. Most everyone understood that it was socially unacceptable to air your dirty laundry or family skeletons are best kept in the closet. Some families have walk-in closets full of skeletons and as a society, we are opening the doors and windows and letting the skeletons out. As well intended as such advice may have seemed, suppressing truth not only isolates, but also manifests in anxiety, depression and even physical illness. What we now clearly understand in the therapeutic world is that it is damaging to the body when secrets are kept because when we are at war with ourselves and our story, we are causing anxiety and stress. Examples of the harm of such secrecy and avoidance can be found in looking back at previous attitudes towards closed adoptions and the experiences of World War II veterans.

Time has shown that when war veterans withhold their stories, it often contributes to emotional turmoil. This is damaging to the soul and spirit. I became more aware of this unspoken code—the belief that sharing vulnerable stories is a sign of weakness—when one of my sons interviewed World War II veterans for his Eagle Scout project. At the time of his project, the *Library of Congress* was urgently seeking verbal recordings of those who served in the war since that generation of soldiers was quickly passing away. My son was able to find ten veterans willing to participate. As I sat with my son listening to their interviews, I felt honored. Their stories were filled with deep trauma. Each man shared horrific events they witnessed or taken part of. They experienced fear during wartime. One veteran shared that after the atomic bomb dropped in Hiroshima, Japan, part of his job was to collect the bodies out of trees. Another soldier talked about surviving in shark-infested waters after his ship went down in the Pacific. Human resilience to endure such difficult life events is awe-inspiring.

The most shocking part of the interviews was when the veterans revealed that they had *never shared their stories,* not even with their own families. It felt like there was an unspoken rule that when they returned home, they needed to leave the past in the past. Today, we understand that healing requires us to feel our emotions and take ownership of our experiences. The unfortunate fallout from not allowing the mind and body to heal properly is that the body can attempt to drown the story with substance use, anger, or other maladaptive behaviors.

Finding Answers

If you know there are parts or pieces of your story or an experience that feels unclear or unanswered, I encourage you to continue to keep putting the pieces together. The process might include working on your family history, writing a letter to your abuser about how you felt (even if you never send it), returning to the place where the trauma occurred, speaking to emergency personnel who were on the scene, or asking questions of someone who might hold the answers. What do you need to understand your story? What is your body asking for to continue healing?

Part of the story I needed to put together from my childhood was learning more about my biological father's life. Even though he never showed interest in meeting me, I felt drawn to understand who he was and learn more about his family line. I could not ask him directly, as he passed from a traumatic accident when he was only 26 years old and I was just 4 years old. I looked to other sources. I read police reports, newspaper articles, and obituaries that described the details of his death, which occurred from falling while climbing a canyon cliff after his raft burst on the Boise River in Idaho. I hired a genealogist to learn more about his family line. Eventually I connected with relatives through the yellow pages and later through DNA testing. This journey was important to me. I had longed for the answers and didn't feel at peace until I went through the process. Everyone is different, someone else might feel better not knowing such information. Each person's needs and journey will look different.

Witnessing the profound emotional and physical change in a client when they claim their story is truly remarkable. Through the years, I have had clients share heavy and heartbreaking experiences and memories they had never shared with anyone. Some of these experiences occurred decades earlier. The raw emotions that are released with the story reveal the intense pain and hurt that was bottled up. As the story is shared, processed, and claimed, peace settles into the body and soul. It is a brave journey, but undeniably worth it.

When we claim our story and are at peace with it, we are taking the wheel and driving our own car. I want you to take control of your story. There is no reason your story should control you. Even in the midst of a hard, and messy story, beauty and calmness can be found in clarity and truth. You have the pen, you have the voice, and you have the tools. Remember: "Your heartache is someone else's hope. If you make it through, somebody else is going to make it through. Tell your story."[5] By sharing pieces of my story, I hope it will help you in your healing journey. You are headed for the *Sunshine Phase*. You are strong!

Activities

1. Assess if you have accepted and shared your story. If not, find someone you feel comfortable sharing your story with.
2. Do you need more answers to complete your story, like I did with my birth father? If so, make a plan to see if you can find the answers.
3. Is there someone in your trauma story you would like to express your feelings to? If so, this would be an effective therapeutic project to work with a therapist.

Sources

1 Van Der Kolk, M.D., B. (2020, November 29). *Breaking the silence.* Maria Shriver. https://mariashriver.com/breaking-the-silence/

2 Brown, B. (2023, November 14). *The Gifts of Imperfection | Owning our story and loving ourselves through that process is the bravest thing we'll ever do. - Brené Brown.* Brené Brown. https://brenebrown.com/art/tgoi-owning-our-story/

3 Van Der Kolk, B. A. (2015). *The body keeps the score: Brain, Mind, and Body in the Healing of Trauma.* Penguin Books. p.13

4 Van Der Kolk, B. A. (2015). *The body keeps the score: Brain, Mind, and Body in the Healing of Trauma.* Penguin Books.

5 McManus, K., Williamson, J. (2018, November 23). 20 Quotes about Sharing Your Story, Baring Your Heart & Healing Hurts. *Healing Brave.* https://healingbrave.com/blogs/all/quotes-about-sharing-your-story

CHAPTER 40

HOPE

Finding Light in the Darkness

Hope is like the sun, which, as we journey toward it, casts the shadow of our burden behind us.

— Samuel Smiles

It isn't easy to accept that the healing process takes time and some injuries may last a lifetime—or at least take years to work through. Like most trauma survivors, since the day of my *Trauma Storm,* I had a yearning for a magic wand to put me back to the way I used to be. I miss the stability of being emotionally regulated without trauma triggers. There are still moments of sadness when I reflect on the loss. Somethings will never return to the way they were. These moments bring deep grief because of the scars left by trauma. Nevertheless, there is much hope in knowing that the *Trauma Storm* does not define my story, my dreams, my future, or me. Yes, working through the *Trauma Impact Phases* will always be part of my story, but I am so much more than that event. I claim me. Hope lies within my own power.

With time and intentional effort, healing transformations will happen. Life can still offer beauty, new opportunities, meaningful connections, peace, and even joy. There is hope.

The Trauma Storm Phase: The Loss of the Iconic Twin Towers

In the 1980s and 1990s, I lived on the East Coast and visited New York City often. Whether on family vacations, road trips, or visiting my dad when his ship was in port, I always looked forward to being in the city. The World Trade Center's Twin Towers were known around the world. I remember going inside, seeing the rows of escalators, the elevator banks and riding all the way to the top of World Trade Center's Twin Towers. The towers were iconic. No one could have imagined they would someday vanish from the New York City skyline, let alone collapse in such a traumatic way on September 11, 2001.

Thinking of it in terms of *Trauma Impact Phases,* the *Storm Phase* of the September 11 attacks began the day the towers fell. During the unnerving days that followed, people in the United States froze. The tri-state area, especially, felt devastated, fearful, and hopeless. The combined loss of life, livelihoods, and destruction of property was incomprehensible. In the days that followed, it was impossible to imagine that the space where the towers once stood could ever feel beautiful, safe, and hopeful again. As with any traumatic event, it can be hard to believe it really happened. One sign of the *Trauma Storm Phase* is adjusting to a new reality. Every fiber of your being wants it to be a bad dream, hoping life will return to the way it used to be.

Over the years, whenever I traveled to New York City for meetings at the *United Nations,* I would visit Ground Zero, where the towers once stood. My first visit came just a couple of months after the devastation. Flowers, pictures, and heart-wrenching notes of love lined the chain-link fence, as mourners paid their final respects. Large piles of dirt and rubble served as a stark reminder of the tragedy. There was a somber feeling in the air. The whole city seemed to mourn. The city felt different—quieter, carrying a shared grief. On each subsequent visit, I could see the phases of the trauma unfold. From the day of the attacks and the weeks after, it was the *Storm Phase*—nothing made sense, nothing felt safe, and nothing seemed right.

The Clearing Phase and Signs of Hope

As I continued to visit in the years that followed, it felt like the the *Clearing Phase.* With each visit, I observed the process of rebuilding. It started with clearing the debris, digging down to the foundation, removing the nearly unrecognizable remnants of what once was an iconic landmark.

At first, watching the changes was emotionally painful, but over time, I began to feel excited to see the changes and the new building. Even the atmosphere in the city began to shift. I noticed the city's energy becoming more alive and hopeful. One of the healing symbols was called the *Tribute of Light,* two blue shafts of light pointing into the sky to honor the lives lost that fateful day. The *Tribute of Light* could be seen as far as sixty miles away.[1] Chapter 4, *The Decision to Rebuild,* discusses the many cities and buildings that have been rebuilt from the ashes of destruction. Likewise, a decision was made to rebuild the World Trade Center.

Over the next decade, the sight of the World Trade Center and surrounding blocks were transformed into the stunning One World Tower, which stands 104 stories tall. It is now a beacon in the city, along with two striking memorial pools representing the footprint of the Twin Towers.[2] The transformation of the landscape and the rebuilding marks a move into the *Sunshine Phase.* While the area looks different and the scars of loss remain, the space now feels beautiful, safe, and hopeful. It feels like a sacred space. It feels like the sun is shining. On my most recent visit, I could feel my heart and soul fill with warmth and gratitude for the power of hope and resilience.

A Journey of Rebuilding

The process of rebuilding the Twin Towers mirrors the journey we go through when healing from trauma and walk through the *Trauma Impact Phases* —the *Storm, Clearing,* and *Sunshine Phases.* As my story unfolds, I have hope. I find myself crying less, I have greater confidence in my abilities along with more control over my thoughts and feelings. I am back in the driver's seat. I feel excited to live life and experience all that still lies ahead.

Constance Scharff, Ph.D., a mental health author and widely recognized speaker, said:

> *Hope is a necessary and powerful tool for resolving mental health issues such as addiction, trauma, depression, and anxiety. Hope can provide individuals with the strength and motivation to overcome*

> *their challenges and persevere through difficult times. Hope is associated with improved outcomes in mental health treatment, including reduced symptoms and improved quality of life.*[3]

Trauma forces the belief that life will never improve, never feel better, will never change, and that much is out of our control. It can be hard to believe that the darkness, chaos, and destruction of the traumatic event will ever be replaced with light, order, and control. That's when it's important to seek out hopeful stories—whether from your own circle, community, or from history, such as the rebuilding of the Twin Towers.

Throughout this book, I have mentioned how my profession has given me a front-row seat to watching lives transform and given other examples in the world and communities. Every story contains moments of hope and beauty, even in the darkest times.

One story that stands out in my life comes from a favorite book, *The Daffodil Principle* by Jaroldeen Asplund Edwards.[4] She tells the true story of how intentional transformation can change lives. The book's headline, "One woman, two hands, one bulb at a time," perfectly captures the spirit of her work.

> *Over 35 years, Gene Bauer planted 50,000 daffodil bulbs, one by one, creating an endless field of daffodils. Her day-to-day efforts resulted in a stunning field of beauty. Through her intentional work, she transformed the landscape, inviting visitors to her fields during the blooming season, which lasted three weeks of each year. It took her time and effort, but she created something truly wonderful—a bright and beautiful field that grew with each passing year. That, too can be the story of our healing! No one knows what it looked like before it had been transformed. Perhaps the field was unsightly and overrun with weeds. Over time, her vision of a beautiful field came to life.*

I love this story because it demonstrates that dedicated, small efforts can change the world. We all have the ability to make the world brighter and better. Our persistent efforts will bring our dreams to life.

If you feel discouraged or can't see how sunshine will ever come again, please hold on to my story, and the stories of renewal that are all around us. I have seen many lives transform as they have gone through the *Storm* to the *Clearing* and finally to the *Sunshine*. Please don't lose hope! Hold on to hope that your life won't always feel the way it does now, and you will have the strength and courage to plant one bulb at a time and see the flowers blossom.

Activities

1. Think of something beautiful you look forward to having in your life.
2. Create a vision board of the world you hope to see in your future.
3. Find a true story of hope and renewal that resonates with you.

Additional Resources

- Podcast: *Stories of Hope* by Major Bryce Davies
- Podcast: *Hope Survives Brain Injury* with Cristabelle Braden
- Podcast: *While We're Waiting - Hope After Child Loss*
- Read More about Gene Bauer: https://www.deseret.com/2010/3/4/20099989/forever-blooming-amazing-daffodil-garden-is-closed-but-her-serigraphs-are-alive-in-a-new-book

Sources

1 The Lemelson Center for the Study of Invention and Innovation.(n.d.) Twin towers of living light. *Smithsonian Institution.* https://invention, .si.edu/invention-stories-twin-towers-living-light

2 History.com Editors, (June 18, 2024) World trade center. *History.* https;//www.history.com/topics/landmarks/world-trade-center

3 Scharff, C., PhD. (2023, May 16). Being hopeful can improve mental health treatment outcomes. *Psychology Today.* https://www.psychologytoday.com/us/blog/ending-addiction-for-good/202305/the-healing-power-of-hope

4 Edwards, J. A. (2004). *The Daffodil Principle.* Deseret Book.

CHAPTER 41

JOY
When Joy Returns

After the rain, the sun will reappear.
There is life.
After the pain, the joy will still be here.
— Walt Disney

One of the most important human emotions is joy. Why joy? Why not happiness or another emotion? The answer is backed by science: joy and resilience fuel each other. The more you feel joy, the more resilience you develop, therefore - the more joy you continue to experience.[1]

There is a difference between happiness and joy. You can't be happy and sad at the same time, but you can be sad yet still feel joy. How is that possible? According to Rebekkah Frunzac, M.D., a general surgeon and chief wellness officer at *Mayo Clinic Health System*: "When you are joyful... you appreciate moments of happiness within the bigger context of life."[2] Anyone can have a difficult day but still feel joy. Joy is a deeper, more enduring emotion than happiness. Joy points to a higher purpose and can transcend circumstances. You need very little of the world's favor to feel joy. Joyful attitudes are contagious. They spread through your eyes, your attitude and your actions. Joy can exist in the face of hardship, disappointment, or pain.[3]

After the *Storm Phase,* I felt as if I'd lost my joyful spirit. It had always been part of my inherent nature, even during the challenges of my childhood. Now though, for the first time in my life, my joy was gone. In an instant, this traumatic experience erased my ability to be joyful. Trauma can alter our ability to feel and see joy. I had never imagined

I could feel so emotionally drained or colorless. I could not imagine returning to the effortless joy I once felt before the trauma. It was as if someone converted my life from a vibrant, happy one to a grainy, gloomy, forever-muted life.

In this stage, the strange thoughts and inner dialogues feel like desperate attempts to convince yourself that living in such a depleted state might be okay. You reason that a smaller, dimmed-down or lesser life is acceptable, that you can make the best of a hollow future. These conversations don't really make sense, but neither does trauma. Your brain is searching for balance, caught between accepting what is and imagining a future that no longer feels possible. As a very visual person, my world lost all its color and light. Desperately yearning to feel brightness and joy, I wondered if life would ever feel normal again. Would real joy return? It was a real battle—emotionally, mentally and spiritually.

I wanted to believe that good things could happen. It became more than a goal or a wish—those thoughts marked a defining moment of my life. Matching the discouragement with determination, I committed to "fight like hell for peace and joy." The words *"fight for peace and joy"* became my anthem of strength and personal fight song!

Intentional Effort

After surviving the *Storm Phase* and heading into the *Clearing Phase*, I began to intentionally seek meaningful, joyful moments. One of those is captured in the photo on the back cover of this book. Before the trauma, pausing to admire a flower was second nature. But on that summer day, I was deliberately reclaiming my life. My healing required conscious effort.

Riding my bike beneath the Wasatch Front, I let myself notice every detail—the horses grazing in the field, and the wildflowers that dotted the path. The picture-perfect day offered more than beauty—it was mending my soul. My mind and body were relearning how to feel joy and happiness again. I refuse to live my life seeing the world through darkened glasses, I wanted it to be clear and bright. A saying my Aunt loves is: "Even on my darkest day, I want to be like a sunflower and stand tall and face the sun."

Remarkably, there are many proven health benefits to capturing joy. In a six-decade-long study on the emotions of 180 Catholic nuns based on their diaries, the nuns who were positive and joyful were found to live much longer lives.[4] If seeking joy doesn't come naturally, it can be learned. A study at the *University College London (UCL)* centered on participants' expectations. Whatever they expected is most likely what they found. If they looked for negativity, that is what participants found. Those who expected positive outcomes most often found them. We find what we seek. Let's seek joy!

Bringing joy back into life after a trauma is transformative and can look different for everyone. Think about what brings you joy. For one person, it could be hiking, another going to a museum, or for another taking a trip. Perhaps it's playing at the park with your child or picking up a past talent that has been dormant. Learning to pay attention to our bodies and find which activities bring us joy and which may bring undue stress will lengthen our lives.[5] There are many different areas we can find joy in, whether through relationships, personal development, employment, animals, nature, art, or more.

In life, there will always be elements that feel out of control. The day I went out for my bike ride, it wasn't perfect, there was air pollution and traffic. I had a choice—focus on the traffic and pollution or focus on the beauty that surrounded me. This can be true as we recover from a trauma. No matter the trauma, we choose the direction of our thoughts.

Intentional Redirection

This is not an easy process, and it requires effort and commitment to choose peace and joy. When I find myself slipping back into negative thoughts and emotions, I intentionally redirect my thoughts.

I know of a woman who felt betrayed by some beloved family members. The situation seemed unfair and disrespectful, especially after all the sacrifices she had made. It was a bitter lesson when she realized they did not value her or the things she had given with them. Daily it consumed her. No matter what she was doing, her mind drifted to the situation, and she would boil with anger and agony. After a year of this suffering, she remembered a class about controlling our thoughts. Tired of the pain, she set a rule for herself. She would allow herself to focus on the betrayal for ten minutes. Then she would intentionally turn her mind to something she loved that brought her joy, like travel, flowers, music, or art. By intentionally reducing the amount of time she was allowed to contemplate the situation, she eventually gained control over her thoughts and was no longer tormented by the situation. It was hard work. She chose joy and it paid off. The intentional effort of changing her focus to joy helped her absorb light, allowing her to eventually rebuild the relationships.

It is similar for me. There are times I allow myself to reflect on the pain for a moment, then I intentionally direct my thoughts back to my happy, grateful, hopeful, and joyful world.

The further away you are from the trauma, the easier this process is. In the *Sunshine Phase,* I feel true joy, happiness, and laughter. I can even belly laugh now, sometimes-even with a snort—which proves I'm truly back to my old self! When I was going through the *Storm* and *Clearing Phase,* I wasn't sure I could ever genuinely experience those feelings again even though I hoped I would. I am grateful that joy is a prevalent emotion in my life now.

When I work with clients, I see a visual change or shift when joy returns—their faces brighten, their energy lifts. While this is not an instant process, it takes time, effort, and patience. I know that this transformation doesn't come easily. But, oh, what a wonderful transformation to witness. Like a flower that seems dead in the winter, we too can bloom again!

Activities

1. Have an intentional "Joy Day" every week. Look for things that bring you joy throughout the day.
2. Make a list of things that bring you joy. Maybe take a photo of a few of them to keep on your phone as a reminder.
3. Perform a small or simple act of kindness that brings you and someone else a joyful moment.

Sources

1 Samudre, N. (2021, December 7). 3 Astonishing Reasons Why Joy is Necessary for Daily Life. *Medium.* https://medium.com/@nealsamudre/joy-necessary-5a3aa73c9093

2 Mayo Clinic Health System. (2023 March 23). *Tips for embracing joy in daily life.* https://www.mayoclinichealthsystem.org/hometown-health/speaking-of-health/tips-for-embracing-joy-in-daily-life

3 Mayo Clinic Health System. (2023 March 23). *Tips for embracing joy in daily life.* https://www.mayoclinichealthsystem.org/hometown-health/speaking-of-health/tips-for-embracing-joy-in-daily-life

4 Danner, D. D., Snowdon, D. A., & Friesen, W. V. (2001). Positive emotions in early life and longevity: Findings from the nun study. *Journal of Personality and Social Psychology, 80*(5), 804–813. https://doi.org/10.1037/0022-3514.80.5.804

5 Danner, D. D., Snowdon, D. A., & Friesen, W. V. (2001). Positive emotions in early life and longevity: Findings from the nun study. *Journal of Personality and Social Psychology, 80*(5), 804–813. https://doi.org/10.1037/0022-3514.80.5.804

CHAPTER 42

PEACE

Holland is Beautiful

Inner peace begins the moment you choose not to allow another person or event to control your emotions.

— Pema Chödrön

In 1985, when I was fourteen years old, my family's world felt like it had been turned upside down. My youngest brother, Carl, was unexpectedly born with Down Syndrome. At the time, the news was devastating to our family. We were filled with a variety of fears, especially after his pediatrician painted a grim picture of his future, listing off all of the things he would never do or accomplish. The doctor even suggested that my parents could place him in a state government home, which seemed like such a disturbing image. Carl was born at a time when children with Down Syndrome were often institutionalized or stayed at home—but never entered the public school system. I had never even met anyone who had Down Syndrome before Carl was born and had only learned about the condition in biology class. As a family, we were concerned about his health, how friends and fam-

ily would react, how time-consuming and difficult his intensive interventions would be, how he would be treated by his peers, and how hard it would be to be the first child with Down Syndrome to integrate into our local school. It was a traumatic time filled with unknowns, sadness, and confusion.

As a family though, we immediately fell in love with Carl. We knew that even though life was going to look different and would be challenging in many ways, this was the path we were on, and we were going to make it the best we could. Shortly after he was born, our family became involved with the Down Syndrome community, which is where I first heard an impactful story called "Welcome to Holland." The message of the story made such an impression that I often reflected on it throughout my life, even when I was going through my traumatic experience. I knew I wanted to share the story with readers, so I reached out to the author Emily Perl Kingsley, who graciously granted permission to share her essay with you:

> *I am often asked to describe the experience of raising a child with a disability - to try to help people who have not shared that unique experience to understand it, to imagine how it would feel. It's like this...*
>
> *When you're going to have a baby, it's like planning a fabulous vacation trip - to Italy. You buy a bunch of guide books and make your wonderful plans. The Coliseum. The Michelangelo David. The gondolas in Venice. You may learn some handy phrases in Italian. It's all very exciting.*
>
> *After months of eager anticipation, the day finally arrives. You pack your bags and off you go. Several hours later, the plane lands. The flight attendant comes in and says, "Welcome to Holland."*
>
> *"Holland?!?" you say. "What do you mean Holland?? I signed up for Italy! I'm supposed to be in Italy. All my life I've dreamed of going to Italy."*
>
> *But there's been a change in the flight plan. They've landed in Holland and there you must stay.*

> *The important thing is that they haven't taken you to a horrible, disgusting, filthy place, full of pestilence, famine and disease. It's just a different place.*
>
> *So you must go out and buy new guide books. And you must learn a whole new language. And you will meet a whole new group of people you would never have met.*
>
> *It's just a different place. It's slower-paced than Italy, less flashy than Italy. But after you've been there for a while and you catch your breath, you look around.... and you begin to notice that Holland has windmills....and Holland has tulips. Holland even has Rembrandts.*
>
> *But everyone you know is busy coming and going from Italy... and they're all bragging about what a wonderful time they had there. And for the rest of your life, you will say, "Yes, that's where I was supposed to go. That's what I had planned."*
>
> *And the pain of that will never, ever, ever, ever go away... because the loss of that dream is a very very significant loss.*
>
> *But... if you spend your life mourning the fact that you didn't get to Italy, you may never be free to enjoy the very special, the very lovely things ... about Holland.*[1]

I believe Emily's story resonates with all who have experienced a traumatic event that has detoured a life plan or destination. There is an adjustment period, a recalibration of your mindset, and the creation of a new plan. There will be things missed and sadness for what "could have been," but the new path can have many wonderful things and experiences. Peace can be experienced in Holland even though it was an unexpected destination.

Finding and creating peace is an intentional action. I have great admiration for former First Lady Eleanor Roosevelt, who was a doer and made such an incredible impact on lives around the world through her humanitarianism and desire for peace. She said, "It isn't enough to talk about peace. One must believe in it. And it isn't enough to believe in it. One must work at it."[2] This is true for world peace, but also for inner peace. One must desire it and work toward it. Like joy, we must make intentional efforts to find peace in our lives. Someone once explained that peace of mind is not the absence of conflict from life, but the ability to cope with it.

My desire for my brother was that his path would be filled with peace and beautiful moments even despite the trials he would have to endure and overcome. As Carl prepared to enter elementary school, I was in my senior year of high school and working on my Gold Award, which is the highest honor attainable to Girl Scouts. For my community service project, I chose a project that would promote a peaceful transition for my brother into the school system and hopefully ease fears the students in the elementary school might have regarding their peers with disabilities. For the project, I set up a Disability Awareness Week at the school. There were a variety of activities students could participate in to learn about specific disabilities. They were able to play wheelchair basketball, read books in braille, and interact with my brother and another incoming student who had severe disabilities and used a wheelchair. One of the activities included the children having the opportunity to ask questions about the two new students, talk with their moms, and interact with Carl and the other boy. By the end of the day, the students let go of their fears and were coming up to my brother and the other student to meet them and give them hugs. My purpose in planning this activity was to intentionally reduce fears and bring peace into the community. *Peace is the opposite of fear.*

My family's path that led us to "Holland" unfolded some incredible blessings, taught us new things, made us better human beings, introduced us to a wonderful community, and brought us a great amount of love and joy. Sure, there have been some challenges along the way, but what felt like a traumatic event at the beginning of the story unfolded into incredible blessings. Carl has taught our family more than we have ever taught him. Carl, who likes to be called "Commander," will be turning 40 years old at the time of this writing and has lived a beautiful and influential life. If you ever want to watch something to cheer you up, look up a TV show called *Random Acts* on YouTube. You can find an episode Carl was on by searching for "*Surprise Recording Session with Alex Boyé - Random Acts (The Commander)*".[3]

How wonderful is it when we can say we feel at peace, even after we have experienced trauma. It doesn't come right away, but with time and intentional effort, we can find it. I can say that I feel at peace with my life and story. It has taken years to meet this milestone, but after all the tears, hard work in therapy, shifting to a positive mindset, and the help of other intentional resources—I am here. Of course, there will be a lifetime of mourning some pieces of my life that can never be put back, and there are some lifelong scars, but I am happy, have my confidence restored, and am at peace. There were times I couldn't ever imagine being able to feel that, but it came. Not all at once, but slowly my peace was rebuilt.

Peace is the ultimate gift we can give ourselves. To live a life in a peaceful state feels much more desirable than turmoil. I refuse to let the trauma control me. I will choose how to live my life, and *I choose hope, joy, and peace.*

My hope for you as you enter the *Sunshine Phase* is that it will bring you warmth and comfort, and that hope, joy, and peace will be your foundation for the life you desire and deserve.

Thank you for walking with me.
Now remember, *you've got this*!

Activities

1. List three goals you want to achieve for a peaceful life.
2. Create a roadmap for one of these goals.
3. Starting today, determine a time and plan for how you will take your first step toward this goal.

Sources

1 © 1987 by Emily Perl Kingsley. All rights reserved. Reprinted by permission of the author.

2 *"It isn't enough to talk about peace. One must believe in it. And it isn't enough to believe in it. One must work at it." —Eleanor Roosevelt.* (n.d.). The Foundation for a Better Life. https://www.passiton.com/inspirational-quotes/7582-it-isn-t-enough-to-talk-about-peace-one-must

3 Random Acts. (2019, February 25). *Surprise Recording Session with Alex Boyé - Random Acts* [Video]. YouTube. https://www.youtube.com/watch?v=3QptTWrcQHY

What are your thoughts from this Phase?

What would you like to change or implement moving forward?

To connect, please follow us on our socials:

@WalkWithKelli

To find more ways in which we can connect, please visit the website where you can find information about:

Online & In-Person Training
Life Coaching
Therapy
Speaking Engagements
Upcoming Events

WalkWithKelli.com

Kelli Houghton Anderson

What began as two young moms organizing a carpool for our elementary-aged kids grew into a life-long friendship. For over two decades, we have laughed with each other through our challenging times. We never planned to be co-authors but are certainly grateful we can continue to work on projects together and hope we can make others' paths easier.

Kelli's passion for improving lives has taken her across the globe, working with International non-profit organizations. As a young girl, she received the Outstanding Service Award for New England in the Miss TEEN pageant. Whether serving as a member of an NGO attending the United Nations' Human Rights meetings, or speaking to international audiences, Kelli strives to make the world a better place through trauma relief. She has found herself in Africa working on humanitarian projects, and in Colombia as part of the movement to stop human trafficking. In addition to her humanitarian work, Kelli has supported trauma patients in private practice, providing individualized care tailored to patients' unique needs.

She has also worked in a hospital setting assisting patients with acute trauma crises, applying her expertise in high-pressure environments. As both an international humanitarian and licensed trauma therapist (LCSW), Kelli's breadth and depth of field experience allow her to offer a unique front-row perspective on trauma therapy and the impact of trauma. Kelli is dedicated to honoring the individuality of others and has a deep desire to relieve suffering. Outside of her career, Kelli loves going on adventures with her family and friends, having fun, and dancing. Her most treasured roles are that of wife to her best friend Wayne, mother to her children, whom she admires, and "Gigi" to her adorable grandson.

Teresa Kearl

Teresa is a humorous speaker, writer, and entrepreneur. As founder of Silver Tech Savvy, she uses wit and positive psychology in her workshops to help technology novices protect themselves against fraud. Her unique perspective, shaped by a bachelor's degree in psychology and a master's in cybersecurity and information assurance, allows Teresa to transform technical subjects into relatable and memorable content.

Outside of her professional work, Teresa cherishes time spent with her husband, children, their spouses, and thirteen grandchildren. Whether solving technical dilemmas or making her grandkids laugh, she brings the same enthusiasm and dedication to all aspects of her life. Embracing life with happiness and humor, she often shares that her lifelong goal is to never be on the evening news.

Made in United States
Troutdale, OR
04/27/2025

30937777R00159